THE
CULTING
OF
BRANDS

THE
CULTING
OF
BRANDS

When Customers

Become

True Believers

Douglas Atkin

PORTFOLIO

PORTFOLIO
Published by the Penguin Group
Penguin Group (USA) Inc., 375 Hudson Street, New York, New York 10014, U.S.A.
Penguin Books Ltd, 80 Strand, London WC2R 0RL, England
Penguin Books Australia Ltd, 250 Camberwell Road, Camberwell, Victoria 3124, Australia
Penguin Books Canada Ltd, 10 Alcorn Avenue, Toronto, Ontario, Canada M4V 3B2
Penguin Books India (P) Ltd, 11 Community Centre, Panchsheel Park,
New Delhi – 110 017, India
Penguin Group (NZ), cnr Airborne and Rosedale Roads, Albany,
Auckland 1310, New Zealand
Penguin Books (South Africa) (Pty) Ltd, 24 Sturdee Avenue, Rosebank,
Johannesburg 2196, South Africa

Penguin Books Ltd, Registered Offices: 80 Strand, London WC2R 0RL, England

First published in 2004 by Portfolio, a member of Penguin Group (USA) Inc.

10 9 8 7 6 5 4 3 2 1

LIBRARY OF CONGRESS CATALOGING IN PUBLICATION DATA
Atkin, Douglas.
The culting of brands : when customers become true believers / Douglas Atkin.
    p.   cm.
Includes index.
ISBN 1-59184-027-9
    1. Brand name products—Marketing—Management.   2. Customer loyalty.   3. Iden-
tity (Psychology)   I. Title.
HF5415.13.A85 2004
658.8'343—dc22   2004044283

This book is printed on acid-free paper. ∞

Printed in the United States of America • Designed by Nancy Resnick

For Matthew, Annie, David, Nigel, and Mark

ACKNOWLEDGMENTS

There are many people to blame for this book, but the guiltiest is Lisa Caputo, president of Women & Co., a division of Citigroup, Inc. It was her idea to publish this material and she made it happen by introducing me to the incomparable Joni Evans. Joni is an Agent Celebre whose charm, intelligence, and reputation make the publishing world her servant. I've certainly become smitten as she doled out encouragement, criticism, and direction at just the right moments. She made all the difference.

Ryan Barton and Patrick Kayser's contributions made all of the difference, too. They'll be famous one day. Doug Garr's advice and experience, for which he is already famous, was invaluable.

What an incredible team at Penguin. Adrian Zackheim is Publisher Celebre and his group has been magnificent. Stephanie Land, editor, has been tactful as she gave her wise comments (it's so easy to be wounded), and Will Weisser has thrown himself into the project.

Douglas Rushkoff, friend and writer, was inspirational at the early stages of this project, as was Dr. Bob Deutsch.

The true heroes of this undertaking are all my colleagues at Merkley Newman Harty. They have uncomplainingly dealt with the distraction that the book has caused. This is especially true of the Planning Department, the best in the country. Super-planners Margot Grover, Janet Oak, and Ann Marie Davis helped directly, as did Hamish Chandra, Jason Cha, and Don Tulanon . . . three highly talented and tail-waggingly keen interns. But the whole group took up the slack with alacrity and delivered performances that made me proud.

My fellow partners, Alex Gellert, Steve Harty, Andy Hirsch, Parry Merkley, Marty Orzio, and Randy Saitta, have been very, very supportive both emotionally and by providing the actual resources that got this job done.

And finally, I must thank the most uncomplaining, motivating, and insightful book widow ever: Matthew.

CONTENTS

Contents

INTRODUCTION

That there was a possible connection between cults and brands became more and more apparent to me as I watched people at a research facility on a cold night in New York. Eight customers had been asked to share their feelings about a well-known brand of sneaker. These eight individuals expressed the kind of intense conviction I had only imagined possible at a revivalist meeting or cult gathering. Their language verged on evangelical; their passion was on the brink of zealotry. They were converts.

What I was watching was ironic considering that I had just come from a meeting of anxious marketers who had been fretting that brand loyalty was dead. There were too many products, and they were too much the same. The consumer was king and marketers were servants reduced to begging for a scrap of attention to be paid to their brand before customers moved on to the next. These hand-wringers clearly hadn't met the consumers I was watching in that research room.

Where did that kind of cultlike devotion come from? How can anyone venerate something as banal as footwear? Can that kind of commitment be reproduced for other brands? Perhaps, I wondered, the answers to these questions could be found by studying the ultimate expression of devotion, the kind that is found in cults. If these people had *cultlike* devotion, then why not look at the original, *cult devotion?* How do cults generate such famously intense attachment? How do the few cult brands that exist create strong commitment? Are the dynamics of attraction essentially the same? And if so, are the techniques that create that degree of devotion transferable between the two?

I resolved that night to try and answer these questions by researching organizations that appeared to breed cultlike attraction, whether they existed in the sacred or secular realms. In the years that followed I met members of cults both famous and furtive; I met CEOs of companies and the brand addicts they had nurtured; I met with soldiers, Trekkies, fans, and cult deprogrammers. A Mac user told me that "PC users must be saved" and a young cult member insisted that his religion is a "brand."

ISN'T THIS EXERCISE FAR-FETCHED, EVEN UNETHICAL?

Aren't cults manipulative, evil organizations intent on exploiting the gullible? Should they be a source of insight for commercial gain? In any case perhaps the insights are not transferable. And isn't it a little implausible to believe that anyone, at least on a large scale, will attach themselves to a brand with the same devotion as a religion? Surely the sacred and the profane should, and really do occupy separate worlds.

Let's look at the last point first. The worlds of the sacred and profane are coming closer together whether we like it or not. And much of this initiative is being taken by religious organizations. So-called Mega-churches (there are over seven hundred in America today with three million members), are building shopping malls so the unbaptised can browse their religion after browsing the clothing rack, or fitness clubs so they can have a spiritual workout after their physical one.[1] Some of the flourishing evangelical churches employ classic marketing programs to attract new "customers" using advertising, mailshots, and e-mails. The same type of marketing data that Wal-Mart or Target might use to place stores in underserved neighborhoods is used by some religions to site new churches.

This move to employ secular and commercial tools is perhaps not surprising as the religious world looks jealously at the commitment brands are able to generate. Many religions would envy the "tent-meeting" that Saturn rallied when forty-five thousand owners turned up at the factory for the week long "Homecoming." The volume of "Amens" and shouts of affirmation during one of Steve Jobs's speeches at Macworld suggests a meeting of evangelists praising the Lord rather than cries of enthusiasm for a new hard drive.

However the real point about merging the secular and the sacred became clearer the more research I did. *The same dynamics are at play behind the attraction to brands and cults.* They may vary in degree of strength (although not always), but not in type. When you consider this for a moment, it is not surprising. When research subjects were recounting their reasons for joining and committing, they were describing the profound urges to belong, make meaning, feel secure, have order within chaos, and create identity. This is the stuff of the human condition. When you are dealing with attraction and the act of buying into something you tend to be dealing in universal constants. All of my interviews, whether with a Mormon, a Krishna follower, a Harley rider, or a Marine, surfaced these essential human needs. The sacred and profane are being bound by the essential desires of human nature, which seeks satisfaction wherever it can.

And more and more opportunities for that satisfaction are being presented by the commercial world. We should not be surprised that as the world becomes more consumerist, so do the institutions that supply community, meaning, and identity.

Let's look briefly at the ethics issue. Is writing this book a morally dubious exercise? Should reading it make you feel ethically queasy? I emphatically believe that it is not, and you should not.

The position of this book is that *cults are a good thing*, that *cults are normal*, and that people join them for *very good reasons*. I invite you to suspend any prejudice that may have been derived from vivid pictures of mass suicides and burning compounds on the front pages of *Time* and *Newsweek*. The popular image of cults is that they are manipulative, destructive, and evil. Some are, clearly, and these tend to be the ones that dominate the headlines whenever they do something that offends our moral norms and our laws. However, the majority of the thousand or so cults in America today never blip the radar of social opprobrium. They get on with the job of providing community and meaning for their members, albeit in an unorthodox way.

And who's to say that unorthodoxy should be censured? Cults have existed for millennia as vital organisms of social evolution. All great religions were once cults. Christianity was but one of several Mystery Cults in the eastern Mediterranean two thousand years ago. It can be argued that a great founding impulse of this country was provided by a cult. The Pilgrims who stepped ashore on Plymouth Rock (a classically mythologized event) were a splinter group of what was considered a dangerous cult in seventeenth-century England called the Separatists.

All great social and religious movements have started with bands of devoted followers chastised for being different. Who knows what small cult existing in America today will become the dominant cultural force in a few centuries' time? A highly controversial (and consequently persecuted) small community in New York State in the nineteenth century started what is now considered to be the next world religion. The growth rate of the Church of

Jesus Christ of Latter-day Saints (more commonly known as the Mormons) is roughly equal to that of Christianity in its early centuries—40 percent per decade.

Cults are a normal, in fact an essential feature of a healthy culture, one that would atrophy without them. And normal people populate them. The insights we derive from cult members, and the techniques used to generate devotion amongst them *are* transferable to a more general context. The people who join cults are most likely to be *like you*. The popular image of cult members is that they are psychologically flawed individuals, gullible and desperate. While some do conform to this image the majority do not. Demographically they tend to be from stable and financially comfortable homes and are above average in intelligence and education. They are, in fact, a desirable target audience.

A moment's thought will suggest that successful cults (the ones we will study) cannot be populated by the socially inept and emotionally disturbed anyway. To grow their membership devotees will have to be attractive enough and have the social wherewithal to proselytize. People in significant numbers are not going to join an organization populated by social failures. They will be drawn to a religion such as the Mormon Church, and a brand such as Saturn, through word of mouth. That mouth has to belong to someone whom potential recruits will trust and respect.

Suspend your prejudice about cult brands, too. They are not necessarily small, niche, and populated by consumers unrepresentative of the larger market. The focus of this book will be on large or market-leading cult brands such as Harley-Davidson, Saturn, Mary Kay, and eBay. The only exceptions will be those brands and organizations that I believe are on their way to leader status by using cult techniques, such as jetBlue. Yes, you can have a large cult brand. Yes, they can be populated by "normal" consumers; no, they need not consist of just leading-edgers.

THE IMPORTANT TOPICS

This book is not just an exercise in examining the *techniques* that can be employed to generate extreme loyalty. It is also about the cult and cult brand members' *motivations, desires,* and *attitudes* that allow those techniques to work in the first place. Why do cult members sacrifice money, time, sometimes their jobs, and the respect of their peers, even their family, to devote themselves to a castigated organization? What makes someone unreasonably committed to a brand?

One person I interviewed spends his Saturdays at a computer store barging into sales assistants' pitches for PCs to sell the buyers Apple instead (he does not work for the store). What does he get out of it? It's clearly not just enthusiasm based on product features. Something else is driving such devotion (another I interviewed would dust off the Macs, switch them on, and move the PC models to the back of the shelf). There have been plenty of books about the service programs and product features that can generate loyalty to a brand. But there have been few that explain the emotional and psychological dynamics of attraction and commitment, the reasons we are drawn to a brand in the first place—without understanding the *why,* the *what* is harder to apply, and so we will study both.

I want to examine the *universal needs* (to belong, to make meaning, to create identity) satisfied by a large range of groups, and analyze the *timeless techniques* applied over centuries to satisfy those needs. My source material covers a whole spectrum of committed groups from the secular and social to the religious and commercial. I talked to members of secret cult organizations, established religions, fading cults, growing cults, sororities, fan clubs, current and ex-Marines, Wiccans, members of the Forum, Deadheads, AA members, people working in strong corporate cultures, and brand addicts whether student, senior executive, or homemaker. I interviewed members of Internet brand communities, service, product, packaged goods, and luxury brand cults. I consulted a leading cult deprogrammer (more properly known as an "exit-counselor"), CEOs of successful cult brand companies, and leaders of cult brand movements.

This is not the entire list. And of course the potential list is endless. I continue to interview what seems an infinite rank of candidates even as this book is going to press. Every time I mentioned this study to anyone they would suggest another source, another cult or cult brand that I simply must examine. However, within the first year or so (I started my research in 1997) it became clear that the insights I was uncovering were common across all the forms of devotion I studied, whether it was a community of Phish members or "The Fellowship of Friends" (a controversial cult based in California). After all, they deal with the stuff of the human condition. They are infinitely relevant and universally applicable.

WHAT IS A CULT?

I should start with a working definition of a cult. Although I drew from a large range of groups, a focus here will be cults and cult brands as case histories of extreme belonging.

It's actually helpful to define a cult by comparing it with a phenomenon with which it's often confused.

- A *cult* is normally a group that embraces new or fundamentally different ideas. Its ideology departs significantly from the prevailing beliefs of the surrounding culture. It is therefore *progressive*.
- A *sect* tends to be *retrogressive*. It has separated from

the establishment because of its desire to return to the fundamentals of the established religion. It believes the established religion has compromised its ideology. Hence most fundamentalist groups are sects.

It's worth noting that sociologists of religion have taken to calling cults New Religious Movements (NRMs) in an attempt to distance what they see as perfectly legitimate social phenomena from the popular image that the word *cult* now conjures.

The University of Virginia, a leading academic source of information on new religions has a New Religious Movement homepage. This is from its mission statement:

> Religions and human cultures are constantly being renewed and invigorated. . . . At some point, every religion was new. There are no exceptions. And every vital religion is more or less constantly experiencing movement from within and pressures from the outside to change and adapt.

If we are defining cults it would be an oversight not to include a leading anticult group's description. The AFF (the American Family Foundation) has a long history of anticult activity and was originally founded by parents concerned by their children's (often adult children's) membership of NRMs. Not surprisingly, it's a little negative. It corresponds pretty closely to that held by the general population, and reflects the view that these groups are dangerously aberrant (some obviously are):

> Cult: a group or movement exhibiting a great or *excessive* devotion or dedication to some person, idea or thing, and employing *unethically* manipulative techniques of persuasion and control designed to advance

the goals of the group's leaders, to the actual or possible *detriment* of members, their families or the community. (my emphasis)

For our purposes, and perhaps a little cheekily, I will take this definition and adapt it to define the more typical cult, ones not associated in the popular mind with psychotic leaders and damaged members:

> **Cult:** a group or movement exhibiting a great devotion or dedication to some person, idea, or thing. Its ideology is distinctive and it has a well-defined and committed community. It enjoys exclusive devotion (that is, not shared with another group), and its members often become voluntary advocates.

By extension the same would define a cult brand:

> **Cult Brand:** a brand for which a group of customers exhibit a great devotion or dedication. Its ideology is distinctive and it has a well-defined and committed community. It enjoys exclusive devotion (that is, not shared with another brand in the same category), and its members often become voluntary advocates.

There are as many definitions as there are interested parties, but this will serve us well enough. You'll note that some key distinctions common to the brand and cult definitions are the ideas of community and belonging, ideology, devotion, and advocacy. All these will be explored in great detail in the following chapters.

THE
CULTING
OF
BRANDS

1

THE GREAT CULT PARADOX:
WHY PEOPLE JOIN

What compels sane, stable, intelligent individuals to sacrifice virtually everything? Why do they throw money, time, sometimes their careers, the regard of their peers, and even their families on the altar of cult belonging? Commitment—true commitment—is exclusionary. Devotion to one thing implicitly requires rejection of another. There is an opportunity cost to everything and joining an unorthodox belief system often demands a very high expenditure indeed.

Devotion to a cult brand also can require significant cost. Obviously, the degree of sacrifice is not the same as that of a cult member, but in the context of consumerism, joining a brand can be pricey, and not just in terms of cash. Why does a loyal devotee of jetBlue leave his home in New Jersey to drive past Newark and La Guardia airports, cross two Manhattan bridges and hack across the endless plains of Queens to take a one hour flight from the airline's home base at JFK? (If you don't live in New York just know that most residents would be incredulous at such an act.) Why does Sean, a student, who can't regularly afford his lunch, feel compelled to upgrade his Mac computer every time a new model is launched just because he wants "to support the company"? Why does the same hungry student buy directly from Apple so that "they get all the money"?

Cult members are manipulated by brilliant psychopathic leaders. That is the populist explanation. And it's as poorly reasoned, and as insulting to its members, as is the idea that cult brand members have been brainwashed by cynical corporations. It assumes that consumers of cults and brands alike are bereft of free will and the powers of discrimination. Perhaps they are flawed by poor emotional backgrounds and educational and financial impoverishment. It's almost inevitable that they'll join a cult because of their faulty upbringing and mental instability.

Research contradicts this interpretation—not only my own, but data collected by scientists and sociologists who have studied cult phenomena for decades. Included among the cult members I spoke with were a senior executive in an M&A firm, managers of corporations, homemakers and students, a clinical biologist, and a financial broker. They were on the whole smart, sane individuals, often in highly respectable jobs, well aware of the choice they had made and reasoned defenders of it to detractors. They were otherwise ordinary in every respect. As Steve Hassan, one of the leading cult deprogrammers in the United States admits: "Since my departure from the Moon cult, I have counseled or spoken with more than a thousand former members of cults of all kinds. These people have come from every sort of background and ranged in age from twelve to eighty-five. Although some of them clearly had severe emotional problems before becoming involved, the great majority were stable, intelligent, idealistic people who tended to have good educations and come from respectable families."[1]

Studies of the populations of major cults by religious sociologists report that their memberships generally follow a similar profile. Eileen Barker, a sociologist from the London School of Economics, undertook a large study of the membership of the Unification Church (more famously known as the Moonies) at the height of its popularity.[2] Her data confirmed that of other academics who had profiled other groups. The cult's recruits tended to come from "conventional and highly respectable homes in which traditional values of family life, morality, and decency were upheld. They tended to believe that their parents' relationships were happy or very happy." In terms of demographics, she found that joiners were largely middle class, disproportionately more so than the general population and that they had good academic backgrounds.

So, these people tended not be damaged by broken homes, impoverished, or rendered gullible by ignorance. But were they sane? Were they ripe meat for the vultures that preyed on psychologically vulnerable souls? Barker continues: "[There is a suggestion that] those who become Moonies cannot really be said to be in their right minds because they are particularly passive, pathetic, or suggestible people. But the evidence suggests that, although a few Moonies might fall into this category, the majority do not; indeed, it seems that, while some such people may be drawn to the workshop, it is precisely those whom one might have expected to be the most vulnerable to persuasion who turn out to be non-joiners."

Ah, but perhaps they were unfortunate enough to have been brainwashed. Anyone, whatever his or her mental state, can fall victim to the machinations of the perverted doctors of psychological manipulation. Even if you have somehow squared your conscience and have opened this book relishing the opportunity to brainwash your consumers, or potential cult members, I'm afraid you're in for a disappointment. The technique has long been debunked as a credible tactic to generate sustained commitment to anything, including cults.[3]

Mainly, those who join cults do not do so because they are emotionally, mentally, or intellectually flawed or because failings in their upbringing have propelled them into the arms of a more loving or supportive environment. Or because they have been victims of sinister mind control techniques. They join for reasons that you or I would recognize, find reasonable, and have acted upon ourselves.

Similarly, near total information, decades of collective experience, and vast product choice make it very hard to hoodwink the modern consumer even if you wanted to. Nowadays, it's not unusual to have your carefully crafted brand strategy played back to you by consumers in a focus group. Buyers nowadays tend to be very media and marketing literate (almost 20 percent of all undergraduates received a business management degree in 2000–2001). The techniques to "seduce" the consumer are mostly open to scrutiny by everyone. Even when the marketing techniques are especially clever and elicit extreme devotion, the seller is often praised by those who have been seduced. As one loyal consumer of Snapple said admiringly in a group interview, "We've been bamboozled by The Man and we know it."

Some cult members have undoubtedly been attracted by the charisma of their leaders, and some brand purchasers are surely a little deluded and extreme. But the majority buy into their respective belief systems for very good, very normal reasons and are quite aware of the criteria that informs those decisions.

THE CRUX OF THE PARADOX

The common belief is that people join cults to conform. Actually, the very opposite is true. They join to become more individual. At the heart of the desire to join a cult, in fact any community to which you will become committed, is a paradox. It's the central paradox of cult belonging and the one that destroys this most pervasive of populist myths.

As one cult member unequivocally put it, "Belonging allows the individual to become more himself. You become more you." This is an essential "why" (the central motivation to join and belong) that we need to understand before we apply the multitude of "whats" (the techniques to generate attraction and loyalty) that are derived from it.

How can this possibly be? The mass suicides of the People's Temple and Heaven's Gate cults suggest the destruction of the self, not its development. Even if we put these two extreme (and rare) examples aside, how can belonging to anything result in enhanced individuality?

Actually the paradox is something that almost everyone has experienced at some time. A community of like people implicitly and sometimes explicitly endorses the individual. It's a vital ingredient of the sense of belonging that most crave when they say they are looking for somewhere to "feel at home." It can create an uncritical and even celebratory environment in which the individual can feel confident enough to find and express himself. There is a "safe space" as one cult member said to me, where the inhibitions normally felt among strangers are removed and the barriers to being you are broken with impunity. You may change the company you work for, your neighborhood, social club, and even your friends, to find a place where it is more possible to *be* yourself with people you consider to be more *like* yourself.

The Moonies grasped this concept to use as a recruitment tool during their introductory weekends. They effectively accelerated the paradox. If a prospect showed any interest in the group during a street encounter or any other social contact, they were invited to one of the Moonie camps for a weekend. The focus of the stay was to foster intense interaction between prospects and church members. They played games, sang, and prepared and shared meals together. If the recruit achieved anything (like singing a song) they were praised and complimented. The overwhelming feeling that participants reported was of unequivocal love, and absolute support in everything they did.

The cult paradox dynamic can be looked at in terms of these four basic steps:

1. An individual might have a feeling of *difference,* even *alienation* from the world around them.
2. This leads to *openness* to or *searching* for a more compatible environment.
3. They are likely to feel a sense of *security* or *safety* in a place where one's difference from the outside world is seen as a virtue, not a handicap.
4. This presents the circumstances for *self-actualization* within a group of like-minded others who celebrate the individual for being himself.

The feeling of difference and alienation I'm referring to is not necessarily extreme. Everyone feels at least some separation from the world around him. To not would really indicate that you are some kind of herd animal, perhaps even insane. There can be no sense of self unless you feel somewhat different from the world in which you live.

For some, the sense of separation can be enough to prompt them to search for a place where they "feel at home" or where the meaning system is more in accord with their circumstances at the time. The person may have experienced some trauma: a bereavement, divorce, or accident that prompts them to fundamentally reassess their worldview. For others it can simply be a low-grade dissatisfaction with the status quo. One man explained why he joined a cult: "I believed that life without some other meaning than the day-to-day routine wasn't really worth it, or there just wasn't enough lasting joy and meaning there. . . . I believed there had to be more." These less-distressed people may simply be open to an alternative when it crosses their path. Active searching or more passive openness are the two circumstances that create an opportunity for cult recruitment.

A woman I will call Joanna fell more into the latter camp. Joanna joined a secretive and currently controversial cult called

The Work. She is a successful, attractive, intelligent woman, Catherine Deneuve-ish in appearance. She was fairly typical of many of her urban contemporaries: accomplished but dissatisfied. She had significant responsibility in a major corporation in New York City. However, after years of striving in her career she had begun to feel disconnected from the "the things that were important to me." She had made a series of minor incremental decisions that had brought her to a point that she had never intended.

"I really didn't know how I got where I was," Joanna explained. "I started out as an art major. I was going into the textile design world and then I ended up being a manager of a corporate business. How did I get there? I was not aware of the sequence of events which I think happened more by default than anything else, but I ended up in the spot that I was in."

She realized that she had little in common with her colleagues and she had lost purpose, which for her was intellectual inquiry, ideas, and art. She was introduced to The Work by a girlfriend's boyfriend. The opportunity to reconnect with herself through a group of similar people was attractive enough for her to accept his invitation to attend a "class" in a downtown loft.

It focused on the philosophy of Ouspensky, who taught that most of us allegedly live in a state of "waking sleep," and that man should undertake exercises to force the consciousness to a higher level of awareness. Joanna found the group and this concept intriguing and eventually joined. She stayed for sixteen years (at considerable financial cost and time commitment).

Outside the group was a tolerable but incompatible life. Inside the group, Joanna found "people who shared the same interests, the same values. That was important." She felt a sense of "camaraderie or sense of community." This sense of belonging had a very important effect. "So in this group, although it was structured rather oddly," Joanna explained, "I felt understood, validated, supported. That the things that I was truly interested in were not just poppycock." The "true" unexpressed side of her that had been stifled in a stiff corporate environment was able to flourish within the albeit tight confines of a secretive group.

Joanna's story simply articulates a universal experience. We all have an awareness of our own uniqueness and difference. We might feel uncomfortable or dissatisfied in an environment where it is not recognized and encouraged. Being welcomed into a group where that difference is validated and encouraged by people who are also different, but like ourselves, is a relief and even exciting. This process is recognizable as a human constant, that is, it is common to everyone and is played out daily in all kinds of circumstances whether at work, at a church, in a social group, joining the military or a fraternity, or even buying a brand.

THE CULT BRAND PARADOX

The same paradox can be found at the heart of cult brands. A Mac user I interviewed, a writer, had personal characteristics not unlike those of Joanna's. He's a successful contributor to journals and magazines, articulate, engaging, and bright. Nor was he a typical nerd. Although slightly disheveled and a little bookish, some of the women in the group clearly found him attractive. He told me that "a Mac made me creative. No, actually I was creative to begin with, and in some ways they made me more creative."

This reveals a very intense connection to a brand. Note how his statement echoes the "you become more you" comment that we saw earlier. His association with the Mac fraternity has made him "more himself," he claims. It has taken that part of his identity that he considers his most defining characteristic, his creativity, and accelerated it. That's a pretty important role he has ascribed to a mere brand.

The community that surrounds Apple is typical of contemporary neighborhoods. No longer dependent on geographic proximity, they tend to be defined by a state of mind, or collective conviction. The Apple community is not even defined by the product itself anymore according to one student, Sean, who said, "In a literal sense, it's based around this machine, but it's based around a certain way of thinking."

Apple has built an enviably strong community based on a "certain way of thinking." Apple brand members (and they definitely see themselves as "members," not just buyers) would define themselves by their different attitude to life, and they align that attitude with that of the Apple brand and the others who buy it. Like Joanna, they have gravitated to a community of people that think more alike, and less like the rest of the world.

Apple has cleverly leveraged the feelings associated with the cult paradox described in the steps above to elevate that brand to cult status: alienation and rejection, followed by validation that in turn sets the stage for self-actualization.

Others echo the Apple ethos.

"It's okay to be odd. We're odd too."

"Like, there's nothing wrong with you . . . that you're not considered an asshole . . . that people don't say you're doing that and we're all doing this. It's okay to march to the beat of a different drummer."

Apple has long had a large community of consumers who pride themselves on their nonconformism. They've seen themselves as creative people in an uncreative world and have tended to find what refuge they can in the businesses of architecture, advertising, music, and film, Apple's traditionally strong business base (currently roughly 30 percent of its customers are graphic designers and artists). To these people, Apple's call to challenge the norm has elevated their attachment to the brand beyond the simple desire to buy a clever box of electronics.

"I spent twenty-six of my years not conforming. Why the hell should I start now? The Mac has played a big role in helping me not conform." A loyal user said this when we were talking about the "Think Different" campaign running at the time. It celebrated famous individuals who had gone against the grain, who had been considered eccentric or even weird. Their ideas and their passion, however, had changed the world. The TV, poster, and print ads featured Picasso, Gandhi, Amelia Earhart, Richard Branson, Einstein, Marilyn Monroe, and others. It was a public declaration that their customers were not alone. In fact, they were in a community of heroes. It represented a broadcast endorsement of who they were. As one person said, "It's okay to be strange . . . it's okay to come up with stupid ideas, to be different."

The campaign broadcast validation to those who had always felt different from and uneasy in a world of conformists (as they saw it). It was the mass media equivalent of love-bombing, the technique the Moonies use to overwhelmingly endorse the individuals who attended the recruitment weekends (except perhaps a little more intelligently done). It was a classic use of the modern means of community building for those groups where geography is a barrier to bonding.

Apple CEO Steve Jobs and his advertising agency had latched upon the inherent feelings of difference and alienation of people who had probably felt separate from the rest of their worlds for most of their lives, simply because they leaned more toward the creative or the intellectual. They were the ones picked on at school for not being jocks or cheerleaders, or at least for not wanting to be. The brand made a siren call to those that felt that way and offered a virtual community of like-others. Jobs publicly validated his membership by associating himself and his fans with those heroes of society originally castigated for zigging when the rest zagged.

THE CULT PARADOX IN SISTERHOOD

Jordana is a Wiccan. It's a cult that's enjoyed a resurgence in recent decades. It's said to trace its origins back to the Old Religion of pre-

Christian Europe that was demonized (literally) by the Church into a religion of devil worship and malevolent witches. In her mid-thirties, black-haired, dark-eyed, and animated as she spoke, Jordana appeared like any other engaging woman at ease with herself.

Her road to becoming a Wiccan was long and arduous. Jordana had grown up as a Hasidic Jew, a milieu where there are rarely tighter bonds between family, cultural, spiritual, racial, and community identity. It was one in which, as she grew into a conscious adult, she wished to explore her own identity. Jordana first wanted to become a rabbi. She asked her teachers questions about the role of women in the Torah and the Bible. She probed about Lilith. "They considered these to be dangerous questions. I think I realized that as a woman my participation was [to be] very limited."

Alienation

Her desire to integrate further into this community and to express her blooming identity as a woman was eventually blocked with disastrous results. Jordana said, "You know, as a woman . . . all the education is geared toward being a wife and a mother. And I felt that was too limiting for me. Ultimately what happened, at fifteen-and-a-half, I was excommunicated by a group of Hasidic rabbis. It was a very painful experience for me."

Her community could not reconcile her ambitions for her spirituality with her gender. She interrogated her world and she did not fit. She could not belong. She could not be herself. The insult was profound enough to propel her to the edge of self-destructive behavior. Jordana said, "I was in a lot of trouble at the time. There were many places I could have turned, drugs, discotheques all night, whatever."

Openness

Fortunately she didn't. Nor did she desperately investigate other worldviews in favor of the one she had left. At just the right time however, it seemed that Wicca found her. "I wasn't consciously looking," she said. "I wasn't looking through the Yellow Pages, or flyers saying, 'what is my new religion?' Somehow, this came across my path and I embraced it. Not just the people, but also the teaching."

Belonging

When Jordana joined the Sisterhood of Wicca, she progressed through the four stages of initiation. She described a rite of passage where "it's confrontation time, it's a very difficult phase. There's a lot of stuff in your face and having to deal with and conquer your fears." Jordana's fellow witch Cynthia described how being amongst like-others allowed women to feel secure enough to really expose who they were: "I think there is really incredible strength with my own sisterhood. I've seen a lot of women tear down walls that have been in place and really get to know who they are inside. It's a safe place because they're among women."

Self-Actualization

Jordana became a senior member of the community and has even written books on Wicca. She's proud of her progress and regrets that her family has trouble with her belief system. Her words betray her sense of triumph and vindication at finally being able to have developed herself. She concluded, "I am a Priestess. I am a Rabbi. I am a Rabbi Wicca. So it's happened for me."

A SISTERHOOD OF BRAND SALESWOMEN

The Mary Kay Corporation is a classic example of the paradox within a business, a brand, and some would say, a fully fledged cult (one that enjoyed $1.2 billion in sales in 2001, with more than 850,000 sales consultants in thirty-seven countries). Whichever it is, it provided a context for Paula to flourish. Paula has an open face and an Irish softness about her. She was neatly turned out for our interview in a business suit that matched her long, wavy brown hair. She's in her forties but looks perhaps late thirties. She was proud of her achievements, but she had a self-effacing manner that disarmed one's expectation. I expected a brassy, bullying, overly made-up cosmetics consultant.

Earlier in her career, Paula had worked for a graphics company where she ran its sales department. She had built the unit from five to twenty people and increased its sales from $250,000 to $3 million in two years. She ran her department "her way," which coincided with the company's. Its values were hers. She said, "I believe that if you keep people happy, they're going to work harder, they're going to want to work for you." She grew as a manager within the company as her confidence developed. The company rewarded her with more responsibility and greater flexibility.

There was an implicit recognition between Paula and the company she worked for. She belonged within the value system of the company. Her work community was one in which she felt recognized and endorsed and she flourished.

Alienation

Then everything changed. The owner wanted to retire and sell the company. With an eye to squeezing the juice from the company budget sheet for a plump bottom line, he became "less flexible with my expense account in terms of taking care of my guys." She refused to alter her principles and undermine the group she had built. She "wouldn't change, wouldn't cut back," and continued to motivate and reward her staff. "It was successful, and I didn't see why I needed to change," Paula said. She was fired when she returned from jury duty. "After eight or nine years making a lot of money for them. I was really heartbroken. I was really crushed emotionally. My self-esteem was just shattered."

Openness

She decided to stay home with her two-year-old son. A year later and now more cynical, a worldview crossed her path that coincided with her own, and she seized it. An old high school girlfriend called her and invited her over to sample some Mary Kay products. She was just starting her business and wanted to get her friend's opinion. Paula visited her friend with a "whatever" state of mind. She'd heard Mary Kay was a "nice company" but she assumed the products were old-fashioned and would not suit her skin. Her friend's story about how she could make money while bringing up her family impressed her and so did the products.

Then she heard a little bit more about the company. "The principles of Mary Kay's company were a lot like my own philosophies and principles in running my department," Paula said. "We're expected to encourage and praise people. So it was very, very validating for me. I was a very easy recruit."

Paula's language draws magical significance to her encounter with and entry into the Mary Kay sisterhood. She emphasized that her friend had unknowingly invited her on her birthday. The language of mysticism continues as she describes her conversion experience. "When we initially decide to become Mary Kay consultants, we come into the company," she said, "but then after not very long, Mary Kay comes into us. Then we're really there for life."

This post-rationalization of the encounter as something fated cropped up during every interview we conducted. The self-story is rewritten and retold to confer significance on what appeared at the time to be a random event. It's as if the meeting must transcend the apparent ordinariness of accident in order to bear the weight of the significance in the person's life that the subsequent events conferred.

Paula described one of the regular meetings among sales consultants to which a potential recruit is often invited to introduce them to the company. "She'll sit in. She'll be included. She's not put in an awkward position but she's included and her being there is celebrated. So she feels welcome and important and valuable."

From the first moment, the operating ethos is a free exchange of ideas and tips on how to build your individual businesses. The sales consultants are not competitive with each other. Paula's story is vindicated through the ideological fit between her view on how to run a successful business and that of Mary Kay's.

Belonging

Overwhelmingly impressed by the annual meeting in Dallas, Paula saw an unalloyed generosity and celebration of achievement that made her feel that she was back home. She had finally found a community that she recognized as like herself, and who recognized her as one of them. And the success of Mary Kay appears to be an endorsement of her worldview. She summarizes the experience: "We're not alone. We're definitely in business for ourselves, but we have an amazing network of women all over the country. It's certainly my business but there's so much more. You just have this sisterhood and this sorority, this feeling of belonging and doing, taking care of each other."

Self-Actualization

And what did this sense of belonging do for Paula? Had it changed her? She said she had not been changed, she had been allowed to become more herself. She'd grown into the person she should have been. "All those things I think were there before, but now they're empowered to come out."

Paula's perception was that she had not conformed. Joining Mary Kay meant rediscovering her identity and potential for growth.

Why do people join cults? In these stories we've seen that the organizations Jordana and Paula joined conferred two highly motivational benefits: a community that created a sense of meaning and the possibility to express their true selves. Paula and Jordana both felt that the groups they joined and their embedded worldview allowed them to *become themselves* in a way in which the outside world did not. The core paradox of cults is that "belonging means becoming more me."

2

YOU'RE DIFFERENT, WE'RE DIFFERENT

ults will flatter you. They will make you feel special and individual in a way that you are unlikely to have felt before. They will celebrate the very things that make you feel different from everyone else; the members will get to know you deep down, and they will love you for what they find.

And you will love them. It will feel good to be recognized for who you really are. All the little compromises that you may have made to "get along" in life—the small or large tradeoffs most of us make for social acceptance—will disappear. You can be yourself.

To generate this response cult organizations need to separate themselves from the status quo. They must exist outside the norms of the culture to appeal to those who feel alienated by those norms. The cult will provide a perfect fit. It does this by both recognizing and celebrating its potential membership's difference, and establishing its own. It needs to say "you're different, we're different too."

Now, face your fear. This means that you can't please all of the people all of the time. One of the greatest dreads of marketers is turning off any potential customers. Sometimes it seems like they have a horror of displeasing any living being. Well, to generate cultlike devotion to your brand, the kind of attachment that leads to large profits and word of mouth, you cannot expect to secure every man, woman, and child on the planet. Instead of trying not to alienate anyone, you must target the alienated and simultaneously separate your organization from the mainstream. Harley-Davidson embraces this fact in its brand guidelines document: "Harley Truth #1: 'Harley is not for everyone.' "

Remember, creating a clear sense of separation from "the rest," and appealing to the alienated has not denied Harley-Davidson a huge business success. In fact it has pulled off dominant market leadership with a repeat purchase rate of 95 percent (at an average of $20,000 a bike this is significant). Removing your organization from the status quo does not necessarily condemn it to minor status.

Cult brands don't become successful only by celebrating anti-social values and behavior, like Harley Davidson. Nor does a cult have to appeal to a marginal group of social discontents in order to grow and flourish. Within one of the most conformist institutions on the planet—a bank—lurks a cult in the making. Citigroup, the world's largest financial institution, is partway through a well thought out, carefully crafted effort to nurture a cult brand—one that focuses on the alienation felt by 51 percent of America's population: women. They are generating cultlike attachment to their brand Women & Co. amongst the well-heeled and the socially connected.

Let's look at one of the world's most famous religious cults to illustrate the dynamics of difference. Neena felt very different from her immediate surroundings when she joined the Hare Krishna movement in the mid-1970s. She was looking for people interested in more spiritual lives when she transferred to UC Santa Barbara and was sorely disappointed by the prevalence of sex, drugs, and rock and roll among her fellow students. Having recently become abstinent from such indulgences, she felt she needed friends to help support her decisions. She found those friends when she was introduced to the Krishna movement through an acquaintance at an alternative bookstore. She had found a group that, in stark contrast to the climate of the times, believed spirituality to be a priority in their lives. They didn't drink or eat meat. They followed strict rules of behavior, and performed rituals in their worship of the divine.

After graduation, she moved to the cult's compound, gave away all of her possessions, and wrapped herself into the sari that she was to wear for the next twelve years: "I always wore my sari, I always followed all the principles, I went to all the programs, I chanted all my rounds every day. I mean, I was a really serious follower."

It is an all or nothing commitment to the Krishnas that forces its members to give up their former lives. Most members live in Krishna temples and adopt an ascetic and monastic life. These devotees take on new names and vow to abstain from intoxication, gambling, illicit sexual behavior, and the eating of meat, fish, or eggs. They shed their Western clothes to don traditional Indian robes and carry a set of beads for chanting. The Hare Krishna mantra must be chanted sixteen times a day and every morning members apply clay markings to the forehead and nose as a sign that the body is a temple of the supreme lord. Male devotees shave their heads except for a small tuft of hair at the back that symbolizes surrender to Krishna, their spiritual master.

The Krishna movement has never been fully accepted by American society. The strangeness of its doctrine and the necessity of its devotees to cut off their connections to the outside world have sparked the ire of the establishment. The families of Krishna recruits frequently assume that their children have been kidnapped and brainwashed. In their minds, it is the only plausible explanation for the defection of their children.

But the Krishna community doesn't seem to mind society's scorn. They have a well-defined sense of group identity that very consciously separates itself from the establishment. Neena recalls, "There was a real strong thing about us and them. That, basically, we're good and they're bad. We would talk about how bad the outside world is and how bad the people are, and how nobody out there believes in God, how they're all meat eaters, how they're all going to Hell. Before you met your guru, you were a dog, like literally, that's what they would say."

These black-and-white distinctions translated into a common feeling of superiority among members. A feeling that reached "holier than thou" proportions and climaxed for Neena one day when she was driving on the freeway. "I just believed that everyone else in all the other cars were going to Hell and that I was the only one who knew anything about God on that whole freeway. I felt so sorry for everyone."

Alienated individuals are the raw food of cults and cult brands. They feel different from everyone else. They feel that there is not a "fit" in their present environment, and that prevents them from expressing their true identity. Cults are a home for such people by offering "fit" where the outside world cannot. The individuals are different, and so are the cults. They are a match for each other.

To attract the Neenas of the world, cults and cult brands need to be "beacons of difference." Cults need to cultivate separateness and home in on those who also feel separate. To create a mutual sense of separation your organization will need to:

1. *determine* your potential franchise's sense of difference,
2. *declare* your own difference with doctrine and language,
3. *demarcate* yourself from the outside world, and
4. *demonize* "the other."

The Krishna movement declared their difference with a polarizing ideology. Their movement was clearly demarcated in its doctrine, its members' behavior, and their appearance. And the cult created an acute sense of the other by demonizing it as a world of lost souls (a tendency of many cults).

We will now look at these four D's of difference and examine how some cult brands have successfully employed them.

1. *Determine* Your Franchise's Sense of Difference

Harley-Davidson has capitalized on a feeling of difference felt by enough people to drive it to market leadership. Here's how one Harley rider I spoke to defined it. He said he hated the "rigamarole": "Everyday things. You brush your teeth. You put on your underwear, you go outside. You empty the mailbox. You look through the bills. You go to work, get off at a certain time. You come home; she's got dinner on the table. It's a beautiful night. Maybe I'll watch *Married . . . with Children*, I don't know. That's rigamarole. It's all definitely not me."

Harley is a "pied piper" brand. It calls out to discontents with an accurately pitched song of recognition. It advocates commitment to a community that is familiar in the most profound way possible, one that is aligned with characteristics that the prospect considers are the "real me."

The real me in this case is the individual who feels that he doesn't quite feel at home in the so-called rigamarole of traditional society. At heart he believes he is a rebel. He loves the freedom of the road and the company of others who also feel trapped by suburbia, job, and family. It's taboo not to like those things because they are the sacred cows of society. But that's the point. Harley riders are free and individual. They are the Gullivers who unleash themselves from the bonds of day-to-day-ness.

A Harley rider I spoke with in a focus group described what made them all different: "The 'bad boy.' It's that part inside you that nobody else knows. Whether it's greasing your weezer, or you're out there taking some girl to the limit, or taking the bike to the limit.

21

Because you've got a little thing inside you sitting on this shoulder saying, 'go for it!' Everyone at this table's got the same guy, I know."

It is not quite expressed in these colorful terms in the company's marketing plans, but it is a powerful statement nonetheless of what Harley means to its riders. It's the unifying manifesto of its brotherhood.

The Harley bad boy was first palpably defined by *Life* magazine in its July 21, 1947 issue. On page 31, there was a photograph of a drunk, fat man sitting astride a Harley with two beer bottles in his hands and dozens of empty ones at his feet. The caption underneath only added to the outrage:

> On the Fourth of July weekend four thousand members of a motorcycle club roared into Hollister, California, for a three-day convention. They quickly tired of ordinary motorcycle thrills and turned to more exciting stunts. Racing their vehicles down Main Street and through traffic lights, they rammed into restaurants and bars, breaking furniture and mirrors. Some rested on the curb. Others hardly paused. Police arrested many for drunkenness and indecent exposure but could not restore order. Finally, after two days, the cyclists left with a brazen explanation. "We like to show off. It's just a lot of fun." But Hollister's police chief took a different view. Wailed he, "it's just one hell of a mess."

What started at Hollister was reinforced in the public mind by the Hell's Angels Motorcycle Club and movies like *The Wild One* and *Easy Rider*. Images of chopped Harleys on the open road and black leather became the epitome of the new American rebel.

These icons, and the role of the Hells Angels as unappointed High Priests of the cult (they have never been officially endorsed by the company, but you can be sure the brand manager covertly prays to the god of benevolent serendipity for such outstanding 'product placement'), have communicated to the cult's membership its removal from society.

Here's how Harley *does* express how the brand speaks to the members' sense of separation. The defininition comes from its brand guidebook that's given to all of its communication agencies to ensure "consistent marketing communications . . . that will fit the Company's global image." It outlines ". . . three essential elements to the Harley-Davidson experience, which riders feel for the first time they ride: *the joy of individualism*, the chance to be free, to make choices; *the commitment to adventure*, the opportunity to change, to discover new experiences and emotions; *the reward of fulfillment*, an intense, personal and consuming bond with the bike that means a richer fuller life." I think the rider above expressed it a little more vividly, but it's clear all the same.

The last part of the statement is an acknowledgment by the managers of a large and successful cult brand of the intensity of commitment and the profound role their brand can play in their customer's lives. Note also the commitment to accelerate the sense of each customer's individualism within one of the most cohesive "community" brands in the world. It's an expression of the cult paradox.

2. *Declare* its Difference

You've identified your franchise's source of alienation. Now you need to declare your organization's removal from the status quo in order to be a siren for discontents. And declare it clearly. A Declaration of Difference will be made by your cult's doctrine, its defining belief system. And it will also be made by the nature of the communication between the cult and its members.

23

THE DOCTRINE OF DIFFERENCE

Declaring what you believe should, by implication, declare what you do not. An organization's belief system should proclaim what it holds to be right and true, and equally, either explicitly or implicitly, what it rejects. There is only one God, Jesus was a space traveler (Heaven's Gate), you can baptize the dead (Mormons), God has a feminine and masculine nature (Moonies). Even the ideology of the embryonic United States was framed in the language of separation. The Declaration of *Independence*, both in name and content, overtly removed itself from prevailing world thinking. Framing a clear system of ideas that depart from cultural norms provides the sharpest delineation between the organization and the rest of the world. And it provides a beacon to the disenfranchised.

Most brand doctrines generate as much excitement as wilted cabbage. They are often forged by a corporation's senior officers during expensive offsite retreats. This "brain trust" spends days trying to differentiate their brand by devising their missions, visions, and values. For virtually every example I've seen, the outcome of these retreats has been exactly the same: what was intended to be a bang ended up as a whimper. In the attempt to please everyone and offend no one most of the ideas were compromised, their destiny to be relegated to dusty laminated sheets on cubicle walls and the odd coffee mug in the company kitchen.

Passionate commitment is often in proportion to the strength of the vision and ideas contained within the organization's theology. Members will want to commit to *something*, and the less distinct and the more content-free its belief system, the weaker the buy-in is likely to be.

THE DIALOGUE OF DIFFERENCE

An ideology only gets you so far. It is in the day-to-day interaction between the cult brand and its members that a true bond of difference can be made.

Much of the communication of difference within the Harley community has actually been undertaken not by the manufacturers and marketers of the brand, but by and for its users. The cult brand's identity has been formed over decades by its membership. Consider the focus group that we conducted. Around the table sat an ex-con in need of dental work (he wouldn't give his address), a suit (as the ex-con defined him), an African American (he said he was "sitting around the table with a bunch of white guys, very relaxed"), and several others from diverse backgrounds.

Whether you are a rider who's on the lam, or one who's a lawyer by day and a rebel on the weekend, the singular thread within the Harley community is the desire to express the "bad boy." And where did that bad boy imagery come from? It started on that day in Hollister, it was sealed by the behavior of the Hell's Angels, and reinforced by *Easy Rider* and *The Wild One* and countless media depictions since. The recent management has been smart enough to exploit what has happened serendipitously. The history and the values that the membership itself created have been incorporated into the declaration of difference that the brand now proudly trumpets.

Harley-Davidson has built a huge business on the bad boy. Harley had a dominant market share of 36 percent and sales of $3.3 billion in 2001. In the same year, its market value increased 40 percent while the S&P fell 15 percent. It has an owner's group numbering 640,000. Harley executives have become the envy of many other business people in the United States. They've leveraged their potential and existing customers' sense of alienation and in the process pulled off the creation of a market leader, a mass cult.

3. *Demarcate* the Cult from the Status Quo

Another crucial element in the demonstration of the community's removal are the actions it takes to draw a line in the earth between itself and the rest of the world. They are the daily acts of demarcation. Moonies get married at mass weddings. Jehovah's Witnesses won't accept blood transfusions and refuse to salute the flag. Christian Scientists avoid medicine. Mormons don't drink coffee, tea, or alcohol, or smoke, they wear strange underwear, and really do give 10 percent of their income to the church. Krishna followers are vegetarian, chant a lot, wear saris, and the men shave their heads.

These are the things that immediately separate the cult and its followers from the rest of society. The rituals, appearance, doctrine, and behavior of its members draw a boundary between the cult and the norm.

Simply declaring that "we're different" is obviously not enough for a cult or cult brand. It needs to *be* different. It needs to look and feel distinct for it to be credible to those outside who seek difference and for it to function convincingly for those inside who want to experience difference. In everything it or its membership does the cult needs to demarcate itself by its actions and appearance. The cult needs to separate itself from its surroundings by "living its difference."

How is this done? Many of the tools available have several functions within the cult, of which creating difference is but one. The proper use of ritual, iconography and symbols, rules and regulations, sacred texts, language, and appearance will simultaneously reinforce the memberships' feelings of solidarity, create group identity, communicate its ideology, and encourage advocacy, among other roles, and these will be covered later in the book. But we will look at just a few of these available tools and in this context, examine how they serve to demarcate the cult from the status quo.

An important point is that these tools serve to emphasize the cult's otherness not just by the strangeness of the acts or things themselves, but also by the foreignness of the meaning they carry. They are nearly always manifestations in one form or another of the doctrine of the cult. For example, Krishnas don't eat meat because they believe that such physical indulgences could taint their spiritual quest for Krishna consciousness. Further, the congregational chanting of the Hare Krishna mantra is more than just a community-building exercise. It is believed to be the most effective means of self-purification. Only Mormons can enter some parts of the Temples and only "endowed" members (those who have been qualified as "worthy" and undertaken a ceremony of acceptance) can enter those places where marriages and other vital rituals are performed.

EXCLUSIVITY—NOT EVERYONE QUALIFIES

Limited access draws the most definitive boundaries between a cult and the other. At Harley rallies, certain bars are effectively for members only. In a vivid example of "you're not welcome," Tom, a young and enthusiastic employee of Harley-Davidson, had been fraternizing with the membership earlier in the day, riding his own bike and wearing the distinctive Harley leathers. However, he was rejected by the membership when he walked into a watering hole to relax with what he thought were his fellow bad boys. He had made a critical mistake that night. In some moment of lunacy he chose to wear khakis and a polo for the evening. He walked up to the bar to order a drink and the salty bartender refused to serve him. He said that the whole bar suspected that he was "a cop or something." There was a gap between him and the membership as wide as the Grand Canyon in that bar. It was a replay of those classic scenes in the movies when the bar goes silent and its occupants turn around to look at the outsider with hostile mutterings as he makes the walk of death to the counter in the futile hope he'll be accepted. Tom confessed that, "I think I know, pardon the expression, what it feels like to be a black man at a Klan rally. It was the most uncomfortable experience I'd ever had." Among the three hundred or so people there he even spotted some Hells Angels he'd helped earlier that day. "Here I was. I was not in uniform, and I was not comfortable."

APPEARANCES AREN'T DECEIVING

Tom's demarcation experience also identifies another important delineator: appearance. The Marines, Krishnas, Mormon missionaries, Deadheads, and Trekkies—all, in one way or another, demarcate themselves by their distinctive appearance. Not all cults employ a uniform to separate themselves from the other; some often employ more subtle cues. Garrett, a young Mormon I talked to from Salt Lake City claimed that members of the Church distinguish themselves from the rest of the population by their "countenance." He said, "We consider ourselves to be a happy people." Some wear a "CTR" ring (short for "Choose the Right," a daily caution to the wearer whenever temptation crosses their path). And if members know where to look, it is possible to detect the sacred undergarments bestowed at the endowment ceremony, that are designed to preserve the wearer's modesty. Some cult brands can be more blatant in their members' declarations of allegiance via appearance. Some tattoo brand logos onto their heads, arms, necks, and ankles (Nike and Apple logos are often the most pervasive). Others wear brand T-shirts or have logos stickered on bags, clothing, and cars. An Apple user I spoke to wore an emblazoned bomber jacket with Apple logos plastered everywhere. "I wear that damn thing proudly," he claimed, almost daring me to condemn him for it.

The Harley cult membership has its own distinctive markings. Tattoos, leather, bandannas, beards, and ripped and dirty jeans.

Tom, the employee who was not decked out in the requisite garb that night, described the uniform, and its significance to the wearer. He said, "First of all, it's almost like a school uniform, blue jeans, black leather jacket. It has some individuality, but there's safety and there's comfort in seeing that everyone else is dressed like each other."

The Harley uniform is a flag that declares the cult's outlook on life, and its separateness from the polite society. According to one Harley rider that I talked to, "What we wear is essentially a 'fuck off' to the outside world. It says 'stay away from me' and it does keep people away." In fact, in a moment of startling literalness, he told me that his favorite shirt says, "Fuck off" in huge letters across the entire front. He also intends to buy another shirt that says, "Fuck off, I have enough friends."

Iconography is a critical delineator. Iconography also plays a dual role in separating a cult from the norm. It is a visible mark of distinguishability, whether for a product, or a religion. But it also connotes difference as a carrier of meaning. The cross, the apple, the Harley roar (iconography can also be aural) all infer the cults' various belief systems that distinguish them from those of their environments.

The famous Bar and Shield, according to the Harley Brand Guidelines, is equated to a "design on a knight's battle shield, it is the Harley-Davidson coat of arms." This is the official cult iconography and it certainly connotes the status of being mythic warriors of the road.

But Harley has a wealth of unofficial iconography created by the membership itself. Much of it is specifically designed to distance the cult from society. It repels outsiders by fetishizing society's taboos. Most of it is borrowed from that inner circle of members, the High Priesthood of the cult: the Hells Angels. The ubiquitous skulls and wings that adorn biker's jackets are imitations of the

Hells Angels "Death's Head" (their official symbol of a skull with wings). It's within this upper level of the hierarchy that much of the real meaning system has been created and its associated iconography of the outlaw removes the cult from the culture at large.

Without a doubt, however, Harley's greatest icon is not the bar and shield or the skulls, it is the great Harley roar. According to Graham, another biker that I interviewed, "Everyone knows that sound. You can hear it from three blocks away. People who can't see the difference between bikes can tell which one is a Harley just from the sound." He went on to explain that the Harley sound acts in a very similar manner to the clothes of the Harley rider. "You can ride a Harley quietly or you can ride one loud. I was riding through town last Sunday morning and decided to make some noise and wake some people up. It was great, it was a great 'fuck you.' "

THE SPECIAL ARGOT OF CULTS

Language can provide a sense of solidarity to members and exclusion to outsiders. Just as marketing jargon or "consultant speak" can serve to distance and intimidate those not in the fraternity, cults will have a language which only members will tend to get. To bikers, all of us who drive cars are called "cagers." According to Harley-speak, a "yard shark" is a pet that barrels into the street and tries to take a bike down. An "iron butt" is someone who has ridden a thousand miles in twenty-four hours, and within the Harley community, "pipes and slippers" are bikers who demand respect because of their age.

Krishnas believe in the "samsara" (the eternal cycle of reincarnation) and inherit the "karma" (positive or negative consequences) from the religious works or "dharma" one has or has not performed. The goal of a Krishna's life is to break away from eternal reincarnation and achieve "mukti," or liberation, allowing them to return to the natural state of Krishna consciousness. The only way to achieve mukti is through "bhakti," a state of active worship, service, and devotion to Krishna, the Supreme Being.

Cults such as Harley-Davidson and the Krishnas use language as a means of bonding, conveying meaning and separation. Much like some ethnicities develop distinct dialects that are incomprehensible to foreigners, the language of cults is a tool that serves to delineate the boundaries between those who belong and those who do not.

4. *Demonize* the Other

Pagans, IBM, Islam, Microsoft, the West, Communism and Capitalism, Axes of Evil. They have all been identified as an enemy by communities large and small, whether countries, companies, terrorist groups, or brand communities. Demonization is a highly effective means of creating separation and a distinctive group identity. A threat from an enemy, real or artfully crafted by the community's leadership, will generate solidarity and a potent sense of difference.

Steve Jobs has identified, variously, IBM, Microsoft, Dell, and other PC manufactures as malignant, threatening forces bent on destroying freedom of choice (the choice to buy his computer). Richard Branson has painted "No way BA/AA" on the side of his Virgin Atlantic planes in a swipe at the big carriers' attempts to dominate the skies at the expense of entrepreneurial challenges to their hegemony.

Here is part of a famous speech given by Jobs at Macworld in 1984 to launch the Macintosh. It's an astonishing performance in the art of demonization. He was introducing the commercial that has since been sanctified by the Apple community as defining what Apple is all about. You've seen it, it's the one where a young woman throws a hammer at a screen on which a Big Brother figure is ranting at his oppressed followers. I've reproduced some of the audience's responses to Jobs's Churchillian invocations to fight on the beaches of computer freedom. Their amens recall those heard at an Evangelical church rather than an audience's response to the launch of a box of electronics.

"It is now 1984. It appears IBM wants it all. Apple is perceived to be the only hope to offer IBM a run for its money. Dealers, initially welcoming IBM with open arms now fear an IBM dominated and controlled future. They are increasingly and desperately turning back to Apple as the only force that can ensure their future freedom. IBM wants it all and is aiming its guns on its last obstacle to industry control: Apple. Will Big Blue dominate the entire computer industry? [Shouts of "no!"] The entire information age? ["Never!"] Was George Orwell right about 1984? [More exclamations and cheers]."

The sense of group identity and separation was palpable in the hall that day. Maybe Steve Jobs tilted at windmills during his leadership at Apple. Was IBM really out to get his company? It doesn't matter whether it was or not. Real or imaginary, identifying an enemy and dramatizing a threat will galvanize the community's sense of separation, unity, and identity.

A second very efficient outcome of antagonism is that by defining the other, the cult defines itself. If IBM is characterized as huge, lumbering, dull, and intent on gaining a monopoly, then Apple is agile, creative, and fighting for freedom. If British Airways and American are also huge, unimaginative, malevolent institutions, then Virgin is piratical, fun, and also fighting for freedom. Demonization allows the cult to define itself (and its essential difference) by condemning the other as a photographic negative of itself.

And demonization is versatile. The more usual object of denigration is a thing: a competitive religion or a company such as IBM. But you can also demonize an intangible. You can demonize a state of mind or action. The Christian Church has persecuted other religions in its history of demonization, but it has also created a sense of identity and solidarity by castigating intangibles, such as "worldliness."

Brands can do this, too. Apple has not just demonized Microsoft, but the intangibles of dullness and bullying. Circumstances change, and when Apple realized it was time to form a crucial alliance with Microsoft, its former archenemy, it had to revise its demon. It put its negative emphasis on conformity, which it very effectively dramatized in the "Think Different" campaign.

Intangible demons can allow a cult or brand to dramatize threats that have no time limit on them (conformity will always exist). Intangibles also have no size limit. If Apple ever grew to be the size of Microsoft or IBM, those organizations would lose their credibility as threats to the Mac community. But intangible demons are as large as the human race. Nike can invoke a collective sense of identity as the brand of self-achievement even from its position as market leader by demonizing "not doing it," a fear for millions of fitness conscious consumers.

A cult or cult brand needs to be a siren to those who are discontented with the status quo. To do this well, it needs to identify the source of its potential franchise's sense of separation. This feeling is not limited to the socially or psychologically damaged. Harley-Davidson calls to those trapped by the claustrophobia of the everyday—a feeling we can all identify with at some time. It needs to plumb our deep wells of alienation. To call to the discontented, an organization must remove itself from norms of the culture and declare and demonstrate its separation to those who feel separate.

3

WE LOVE YOU

True and lasting commitment to brands and cults is effected through people. It's all about the "primacy of the person." What do I mean by primacy of the person? The conventional wisdom is that people buy ideas or things. The transaction is between the individual and the object or idea. The religious and political world holds this to be true and so does business. Ask a priest what converts a recruit, and he will say the ideology, "The truth of God's Word." Ask a marketing or advertising executive what a consumer buys and they will claim that it is the carefully crafted ideology of the brand, its essence, its DNA, its brand values, its image. If it's compelling enough the crowds will flock. Or they will gather for the tangible things, the product or service features.

It's easy not to question this conventional wisdom, because the objects of the pitch agree. Ask a convert what converted him and he is likely to say that it was the religion's doctrine. Ask a consumer and he will respond in kind, even passing over the brand ideology to claim that it was the brand's tangible features that seduced him (rarely will anyone claim they buy "image").

In other words, we who are responsible for creating commitment to our brand or religion believe that the content is more important than medium, in this case, the agency of human relationships. It's the idea or the object that seduces, not the people or community that brings it to them.

But we will be handicapping our attempt to build a successful business (or religion) if we settle for these answers or accept the received wisdom of our community. People buy people. Of course, they buy into belief systems, whether religious, political, or those devised for brands. It would be ridiculous to underestimate their importance ... and I don't. (See chapter 7.) And, of course, they consider and enjoy the temporal benefits of each, too. But for real commitment, the recruit and existing members need to feel that they have a relationship with "an other" or "others." The buy-in to the ideology and tangible benefits comes later.

What's the support for this assertion? From the world of cults and religion, my research and others' suggests that the ideology comes later as the object of commitment. Two sociologists made a startling discovery in the Moonie recruitment process: Individuals bought into the group *before* they bought into the ideology, not the other way around. They found that the most successful recruits were the ones who had social relationships with members of the group *before* they joined. The first members of the famous and successful San Francisco branch were friends of the leader, Miss Kim. These friends brought their husbands and wives, who in turn brought their colleagues and friends. When, at a later date, they were asked why they had joined, the recruits predictably claimed that they were convinced by the truths of the cult's ideology. At the time of their first contact with the community, however, the researchers noted that "most of them regarded the religious beliefs of their new friends as quite odd."[1] This person before ideology thesis was confirmed by my own research: "I started going there and I liked it. I liked it a lot because *I liked the people*," said Neena, a member of the Krishna movement. It was the community that she had initially bought into: "There were all those things, everything that goes with bonding. You have the friendship, you have the common activity, and you feel reinforced and supported."

And it's the brands that are recognizing the power of human interaction that are becoming the heroes of business.

IT'S THE PEOPLE, NOT THE PLANES

You can be part of a well funded startup, have all new planes, a cool product, leather seats, live TV, cool snacks. But none of it matters. The people are the brand . . . you are the brand as a person.

— Dave Barger, president and chief operation officer, jetBlue

JetBlue is one of only two airlines making money in the post-9/11 recession and war–dominated world. From nowhere, it has become the wunderkind of an industry convulsing with chronic business-model failure. Its market value, at $1.7 billion, is nearly as large as that of United, American, and Delta combined. Its costs are the lowest in the industry, even lower than those of Southwest. By the end of 2002, its load factor reached an industry high of 83 percent (the average is 71 percent) and its profits leaped 43 percent to $55 million.[2]

Fortunately, the people running the company realize that as important as the substance of the customer experience is (the TV, the comfortable planes, the low prices), it's the *core members* of this rapidly growing cult brand, and their interactions with customers, that are making the difference. It's not the stuff. It's the staff that is driving these results.

PRINCIPLES OF THE PRIMACY
OF THE PERSON

Five important principles comprise the primacy of the person.

1. Recognize and gear your organization to *focus on the person.*
2. Get the *right membership.* There is such a thing as a good and a bad member. A cult or cult brand must discriminate between well-socialized individuals who will engage new prospects, and those who will be unproductive because they are not.
3. Create *opportunities for meeting and interaction* between members and nonmembers. More interactions will lead to more recruits to the brand or cult.
4. Liberate your representatives to focus on interaction. *Remove distractions.* The idea is simply to engage the prospect and make him or her feel good.
5. *Love-bomb.* Overwhelm them with welcome. "Love-bomb" is the epithet given to the technique used by the Moonies at their recruitment weekends. Make a potential recruit feel that he or she is the only important person in the room. Their well-being is the source of yours. It's not about you; it's about them.

Let's examine this in more detail.

1. *Focus* on the Person.

The jetBlue story is all the more remarkable because the airline industry is a poisoned category. Its people are poison and its behaviors are poison. Even Congress, roused by passengers close to revolution, threatened legislation to enforce change. It was the cavalier attitude of the airline management that decreed that it was all right to let passengers sit on the tarmac for six hours without food or drink. It was the "it's not my fault, now sit down" attitude of the staff that sparked indignation from fare-payers. In other words, it was the *failure of the person* that sowed a growing hatred between customer and service deliverer.

"New Air" (the working name for jetBlue in its prelaunch days) believed it should remove itself from the category. "Don't be an airline" was an early suggestion from its first communications agency, Merkley and Partners. The agency reasoned that "New Air" should make the most of its different posture, that it should be a customer advocate in an industry that appeared not to care.

CEO David Neeleman's business model was brilliant in its heresy. Don't follow the route of other low-price carriers and launch with cheap old planes. Be the best-funded start-up in the history of the industry and use the capital to lease brand new aircraft with low running costs and thus competitive price per seat mile. He imitated Southwest's strategy in using underserved airports, and underserved populations, creating markets that competitors could not afford to service.

But the real heresy of the business model was the focus on the person. Neeleman has claimed that he is trying to "put the Humanity back into air travel." Once the fundamentals of the product and pricing were sorted out, the early management team fixated on how jetBlue personnel would bond with the consumer. Interactions with the brand via gate-agents, check in personnel, the 1-800-number staff, and flight attendants would all fail if the personnel were as cavalier as the rest of the industry. The strategy for hiring and training had to be as radical as the functional aspects of the business model.

The management at jetBlue maniacally believe that good employees create good customers, who become as committed as the staff, who feel ownership and even a responsibility to sell the airline to others. In other words, populate the internal cult with the right kind of membership and motivate them to perform, and you will recruit the right kind of membership externally and turn them into advocates.

JetBlue, above all, believes that its airline is a brand. (As David Barger noted of his previous experience at Continental, "I don't think I ever heard the term in the eighteen years that I was there.") Management's constant chorus was that "the jetBlue Brand is its people." Staff interactions were defined by the brand values of "safety, caring, integrity, fun and passion." The concept that an airline is all about humanity, and that humans are the prime vehicle for delivering it—not just comfortable planes—is indoctrinated into the recruit within the very first minutes of their employment.

I was invited to an induction seminar in Miami in early 2002. One of an average of roughly ninety that year, it formed the first day of training for all the flight attendants, ground crew, pilots, head office personnel, and engineers and flight ops. The primacy of the person was made abundantly clear.

Members of the various disciplines were in the same room, a message in itself. The professions are normally rigorously segregated. This is especially true for the pilots, the aristocracy of an airline. Their perception of superior status is expected to be indulged. I could detect their discomfort especially when asked, like everyone else, to stand up and introduce themselves. They clearly felt as if they were in some self-help group and not in the equivalent of "up-front," dealing with higher things. Al Spain, head pilot and head of operations, deliberately punctured this prospect with stories of how he and others crossed the imaginary class barriers in the interest of the customers, such as going down below and retrieving a baby carriage for harassed parents waiting on the jetway at arrival.

This gathering was a symbolic moment meant to reinforce the

collective responsibility to the customer. It was an expression of egalitarianism in the face of the Great Leveler, the customer, that was truly reinforced when management announced that the name given to all jetBlue personnel was *Crew*, whether office worker, flight attendant, gate agent, cleaner, pilot, or chairman.

David Barger, president and COO kicked off the first session saying, "Hey, listen. We're building a brand." Then, he rammed home the preeminence of the person to jetBlue in that formula. "A brand is how you feel, and we're making people feel better by putting humanity back into air travel," he said.

Then pilot guru Al Spain stood up. He is a big, genial guy with several airlines and many years of flying experience. He took the recruits through the development of the name and the design of the brand identity. It's unusual for a company to bother to take its operating staff through a logo and name design process at all, and significant that a pilot was doing it.

The whole morning was an induction into the values of the company, its business model ("designed for recession"), and the focus on the crew ("chasing the experience, not the statistics"). Vincent Stabile, VP of the People Department ran a session that, not surprisingly, focused on the importance of jetBlue personnel. The company may be characterized as a low-fare airline, but that is not what will get repeat customers, he said. It's a trial device, not a retention model: "Low fares will get customers once. Our people will get them again and again."

Finally, Neeleman quietly entered the room as one of the presenters finished. His attempt to be low-key failed, as a chorus of hallelujas trumpeted the arrival of a savior. Cheers, applause, and one or two shouts of "We love you!" rang out. Soft-spoken, shy in his delivery, he described the robustness of the business model. Again, perhaps unusual for an audience of flight attendants, baggage handlers, and cleaners, he gave the kind of detailed presentation normally reserved for analysts, with the same kind of respect for his audience. He finished with a description of what was, in essence, the service profit chain. "Work hard at all points of contact and get repeat customers. You'll make more money; there'll be more profit sharing. You'll feel better with more work satisfaction which means you'll please more customers."

MYTHOLOGIZING THE IMPORTANCE
OF THE PERSON

How can you communicate to the organization the importance of the person beyond simply *saying* that it's important? You can create myths and stories that carry the moral for you. Myths are potent communicators of ideology. They are viral cells that communicate their DNA into the body of the organization effectively because their narrative structure make them compelling. Myths are stories, like any other, but they have a fantastical character to them, transcending beyond the everyday to make a point about the everyday. They are equal measure true event and elaboration, embellished as they are shared and passed along. Just like any story they require a narrative, one that will follow a timeless structure whether told by Homer or Hollywood. There will be a hero or heroine, a challenge, a risk taken to overcome the challenge, and a happy ending. There will be a discovery, or enlightenment, or increased knowledge gained by the hero, and vicariously, by the audience, as he overcomes the challenge; and that will be the substance of the moral.

This may sound intimidating. Does a myth demand a highly dramatic event to make a significant lesson? No, even the smallest things may qualify if they adhere to the structure above. And of course, if they enact a moral within an organization predisposed by the ideology already disseminated by the leadership.

Take the following example. There was a flight delay of four hours at JFK for a trip that should have only taken fifty-five minutes. There was the skulking ogre of heavy fog at the airport, and the queue of airplanes competing for a take-off slot once the weather cleared. Our hero was Al Spain who had a population of restless customers behind him who in any crisis, fairly or not, are likely to blame the airline even if the villain is out of the realm for mortals to control. They were the equivalent of the angry mob with lit torches ready to lynch our hero.

In a small but significant action, Al made his announcements not from the temple of the flight deck but in the cabin, where he took the attendants' microphone and explained the situation in front of the passengers. After several announcements about the persistently bad weather, he finally asked the customers what they would like to do—go back to the gate, or stay in line for a couple more hours and not miss their departure slot. They voted to stay. Back in the cockpit, a flight attendant came forward and said a lady was worried about the people she was meeting in Buffalo. The pilot reached into his bag and pulled out his personal cell phone. He told the attendant to hand it to anyone who needed to make a call. She returned and "laughed as she handed the phone back and said 'you got six calls to Buffalo, two to Beijing, and one to Frankfurt.' And he said, 'Are they happy?' She said 'they're happy,' and I said 'Well that's what matters, right? What's a phone call!'"

When they finally arrived in Buffalo the pilot stood at the door and "people just came up to say 'you guys are great, absolutely great, you're wonderful.' " Despite a horribly long trip a bond had been made to the brand that was stronger than anything that the satellite TV at every seat could have achieved. His actions, and that of the crew, had defused the angry mob and created a small community in that plane. And the event became elevated to the level of a myth because a member of the leadership demonstrated the power of human interaction to resolve a difficult challenge.

One point about the hero. The most potent myths-makers tend to be someone of significance within the organization. They could be the cult leader or one of the disciples or High Priests. They are potent because they create the doctrine by their actions, and because of their status, bless similar actions by its members. They are living ideology makers whose media include their mythologized deeds.

Having said that, potent myths are not the exclusive province of the gods. Ordinary mortals can and do create myths if their actions are extraordinary enough, or the challenge extreme enough, and the moral is consistent enough with the ideology. And of course the leadership will have blessed their actions anyway for it to be a candidate for the culture's mythology.

As the leader of an organization, you cannot guarantee that an event will gain repeatable status within an organization, but you can set up the right conditions for it to occur. And an important first step is to get the right membership of your organization to turn potentially ordinary events into significant ones.

2. Get the *Right* Membership

Socially successful people populate successful cults. The popular perception is quite the opposite. Cults are a refuge for social misfits. Sad, lonely individuals, their fate is to become one of three things: a serial killer ("he was quiet, always kept himself to himself"), an obsessive watcher of *Avengers* and *Doctor Who* episodes, or a cult member.

If cults were really populated by people like this, they would be condemned to be small and inconsequential. They would be hobbled by a membership so shy or socially inadequate that they could not engage others to proselytize their beliefs. What's more, they would be poor representatives of the benefits of belonging. They would not whet the appetite of the prospect.

Successful cults must recruit socially successful people. They must recruit socially *attractive* people, individuals with whom others would want to engage. This kind of membership will be productive in two important ways. They will already have many existing social connections (friends, colleagues, family) to be employed as avenues for recruitment. And they will be socially confident and attractive enough to create new connections easily.

It was summer and Chris was walking down a street in New York when he was approached by "a very attractive girl in a sundress." He had a job in the media and had just finished his masters at a prestigious New York university. An attractive and intelligent man, he was reestablishing his life in New York, having spent some time in Asia following his passion for taking photographs. This woman engaged him in conversation on the street and then invited him to meet some other people in a local bar. He said "why not?" and followed her. The group of people at the bar were "the same kind of people" as he, interested in talking about the same kind of subjects: ideas, philosophy, meaning. To Chris, they were "people I could be friends with, they didn't seem weird in any way. Just completely accommodating."

She intimated that she was part of a larger group of people who studied the kind of issues they had been discussing, but more formally. He was invited to the next group meeting at a loft. "The girl said that if you're not interested you don't have to come."

Note the self-assurance of the girl who approached him. Hardly the actions of a social misfit. She was engaging enough to persuade a complete stranger to come to a bar and meet other strangers. They in turn were immediately attractive to Chris as like-minded, intellectually discriminating individuals who predisposed him to attend his first meeting. At his first few classes he found that he warmed to the group, and despite some of the strangeness of the ideas, felt at home. Accordingly, he related, "I started to have a tremendous amount of fun. I found a community. We talked about many things. People seemed talented and intelligent. There was a whole new system of ideas to get to learn. Some of it sounded preposterous, but I didn't care because there was enough else that made sense. I didn't think you had to buy the whole package to learn something and experiment a little bit. *It quickly became a very intimate experience in a matter of months.*"

The profile of the cult members I met was absolutely consistent with quantitative studies conducted by sociologists who have also found that cult populations are dominated by well educated, pleasant, and socially engaging individuals.[3]

Joanna was more explicit about the recruitment strategy of the cult. Also a member of The Work, she claimed that the cult "didn't want losers." In fact it preselected people of high social status and who were good "connectors": "Very intelligent people. A lot of Ivy league graduates, a lot of professionals, a lot of people who were successful in their field."

LIKE-GET-LIKE

How can you find the right membership, one that is engaging and socially confident? An obvious way, seldom tried by most companies, but one institutionalized by jetBlue and other successful cults, is to get the best staff to recruit others like themselves: like-get-like. Called Peer-Recruiting, pilots find and interview the right kind of pilots, flight attendants look out for people they think could make the grade. JetBlue's agency designed a card to be carried at all times by the crew and handed out to people whom they spotted as likely prospects. They could be a great coffee shop waitress, a checkout clerk at Whole Foods, or just someone they met on a plane or train who was engaging and fun.

THE RIGHT KIND OF *CUSTOMER* MEMBERSHIP

We've talked about finding the right kind of *company* membership: highly personable, strong representatives of the brand values, good recruiters of people like themselves. What about finding the right kind of *customer* membership? They also need to qualify. They should also be recruited by the same standards as the internal membership: quality interactors, reputable representatives of the brand, and good recruiters if the cult is to really grow rapidly. At the end of the day they will become the engines of growth and prime embodiment of the brand. Mary Kay is good at this. Its growth depends on the sociability of its consultants and their customers.

A productive consultant will find highly socially competent prospects. These people will of course have a lively network of friends, family, or colleagues to be exploited as profitable avenues of distribution. The most fruitful way to kick this network into full throttle is to enlist these prospects as hosts for a Mary Kay party. These events turn into highly interactive and fun occasions where existing relationships are fortified, but done so in an environment sponsored by Mary Kay. New relationships are also formed as the participants try out colors and products on each other, also in this sponsored context. These parties are not only an effective venue for selling product, but are also a measure of a customer's interactive value.

The consultant will also be looking out for those who can become consultants themselves. Do they have the potential to create their own profitable transactions on the back of existing social relationships? Do they have the social wherewithal to form new relationships as potential avenues for the brand? And do they fit the profile of the membership, one that buys into the ideology of the brand?

This idea of putting an interactive value on the quality of a cult brand's customer membership is taken literally by eBay. This business model only works through the medium of trust. Both buyer and seller are taking financial and even personal relationship risks by the exchanges they make. The blind auction system of bidding for items that cannot be thoroughly inspected, from people you don't know, and trusting the seller will refund your money if you aren't happy demands a "republic of trust."

EBay clearly lays out its expectations of the nature of its membership, and their interactions, with this doctrine:

> eBay is a community that encourages open and honest communication among all its members. Our community is guided by five fundamental values:
>
> - We believe people are basically good.
> - We believe everyone has something to contribute.
> - We believe that an honest, open environment can bring out the best in people.
> - We recognize and respect everyone as a unique individual.
> - We encourage you to treat others the way you want to be treated.
>
> eBay is firmly committed to these principles. And we believe that community members should also honor them—whether buying, selling, or chatting with eBay friends.

The company has lubricated its transactional model by establishing a rating system for each participant, based on the number of satisfactory exchanges that have taken place. Next to any eBay member's user ID, there is a Feedback Rating in parentheses. For example: Skippy (125) means that this member's User ID is Skippy and he/she has received positive feedback comments from at least 125 other eBay members.

There is also a colored star rating system will tell you how many people have left comments. Feedback from ten to forty-nine people and you get a gold star. Comments from one hundred thousand people or more and you're awarded a red shooting star. Buyers and sellers have a horror of losing their rating. Four counts and you're out. Four bad reviews and you literally have no currency in this market. In effect you are ejected from the city gates if you offend the community's ethical norms.

Like any good cult, eBay has created hierarchies. In this case they are based on abidance to the culture's moral conventions. They also represent one's status as a high volume seller; of course, one is not achievable without the other. The real high performers have been glorified with the term "PowerSellers." As Brian Swette, senior VP of marketing has said, those within this "Merchant Group" are "our strongest evangelists, promoting the company with a vengeance, because eBay's success means their success." EBay has also celebrated them as true representatives of the community's doctrine.

> "As the pillars of our community, PowerSellers are committed to upholding and embracing the core community values that are the very foundation of eBay. They are exemplary members who are held to the highest standards of professionalism, having achieved and maintained a 98 percent positive feedback rating and an excellent sales performance record."

The eBay moral code, the glorification of its strongest adherents, the calibration of its membership base against a measure of quality interactive ability, all encourage the right kind of customer membership. Several of the eBay-ers I interviewed even viewed their rating within the eBay community as a badge of rectitude within the larger culture. There's no reason not to—its code mirrors Judeo-Christian doctrine. And seldom does one get a published measure of one's moral standing, one that's indisputable, based on actual events, rated by participants with no ax to grind. Not until Saint Peter does a tally of our earthly transactions will we get such an accurate reading of moral standards!

3. *Create* opportunities for meeting and interaction

Only Connect!

—E. M. Forster, *Howards End*

The power of the person cannot be overemphasized. It leads conversion, fuels conviction, and modifies behavior. Logic suggests then that we should increase opportunities for people to meet and engage. We should create forums, geographic or virtual, where people can socialize and mix. Members need to interact with each other, but more important, nonmembers need to interact with those already involved. We should encourage, sponsor, and support social ties. These are the bonds that will evolve into strong yokes to the cult or brand. The ties between its members and the recruit will mediate the relationship to the cult or brand. How strongly the member will be fastened to the cult is largely dependent on how strong their relationship is to others within it.

A. Marie Cornwall, while at the University of Minnesota, conducted a breakthrough study on the effects of socialization on bonding to an organization. Her focus (using the Mormon Church as the object of her study) was to examine whether the degree of interaction affected the degree of commitment to the religious belief. And what's more, did all this lead to increased religiously informed behavior? In other words, if you turn up the dial of *interaction,* will it increase the amount of *buy-in?* If you increase the amount of buy-in or conviction, will that have a positive effect on *behavior?*

The responses of 1,874 individuals demonstrated a positive correlation between socialization and belief, and belief and behavior. More socialization leads to more conviction or buy-in. More conviction leads to more behavior that is in line with the belief system. The stronger the "in-group" ties as she called them (the relationships formed within the cult) the stronger the bond to the cult.

Throughout the rest of this book, you will see examples of cults and brands that have created opportunities for interaction, in all its forms, whether actual or virtual.

4. Remove Distractions

Not only should venues for assembly be provided to enable connections, but also distractions should be removed to allow the congregants to form more effective bonds. Liberate the members of your cult to become interactors. Let them become the most effective growth generators of your cult. Let them fulfill the promise of the power of the person.

It's hard to overcome habits of a lifetime. But the wont of thinking linearly is the curse of contemporary business and is too often manifested in the belief that the existing membership are there to do one or both of two things: sell, and/or fulfill functional tasks. Just let go. Don't force your cult members to sell the cult or brand. Don't burden your staff with too many functional tasks. Let your cult members interact. The link to the cult will come later. The Mary Kay consultants we talked to told us that they expressly avoided pushing the sale—because it does not necessarily lead to more sales. The intent of the contact is to form a relationship.

LIBERATION FROM THE SALE
When Saturn was launched, its architects made a major change to the way cars were sold. The industry considered it heresy, and

pundits doomed it to failure. One of the most radical moves was that retailers did not pay their salesmen (sorry, "consultants") commission. They received a salary instead, removing the pressure to close the sale at all costs. The consultant was liberated to listen to the customer. They could offer advice, sometimes recommending a cheaper model if it was in the best interest of the buyer (as happened to one customer I interviewed who was eyeing a more expensive car). In other words they could form a relationship without the venal urgency of making a sale stalking a critical interaction that is the bonding moment between brand and consumer.

Does liberating the member from making the sale work? Saturn enjoyed record sales to become the fastest selling small car in the United States two years after launch, overtaking Ford's Escort in 1995. Was this because the customers were delighted with innovative product features? Were they enraptured by the car's superior design? Customers were highly satisfied. But the source of the satisfaction did not lay entirely in functional benefits, but in relationships. A survey by GM showed that in 1992 Saturn had the highest customer satisfaction rating of any domestic nameplate. Seventy-five percent of that satisfaction had nothing to do with the car, but with the customer attitudes toward the dealer. This positive interaction turned the customers into advocates. By 1993, nearly half of the first-time visitors to a Saturn showroom had been referred by a friend or family member. By 1996 Saturn surpassed all other brands in *sales experience* satisfaction, including luxury names such as Lexus. Not unlike the airline industry, with so much metal around the temptation is to think that product features are the source of devotion between customer and brand. Ultimately, people buy the person not the thing.

LIBERATION FROM THE FUNCTIONAL TASK
JetBlue has structured its business model to liberate its crew from many of the functional tasks of their jobs in order to engage

with customers. For example, those on the frontline of customer interaction—flight attendants—do not serve food. They hand out a limited selection of beverages and snacks (blue chips). Thus they are free to talk and joke with passengers, help them master the in-flight cable TV monitors on the back of each seat, and find pillows and blankets. As the flight approaches its destination, the passengers are asked to share the task of helping clean the plane so that the turn-around time for the next set of customers is reduced.

This last idea is interaction at its best. Customers and staff are all joined in a common and virtuous outcome—the comfort and convenience of the next customer. Being asked to clean a plane, something that would be regarded with astonishment if it were asked by other airlines, has been transformed into a game played with the crew and passengers that can only make the consumer feel good, and part of something bigger. Polls of customers have revealed an immense feeling of goodwill for the airline, in part because of a desire to see something good succeed in a depressing industry landscape. Cleaning the plane becomes an interaction that makes the customer feel part of a joint mission to look after *all* customers' interests in an industry where indifference or abuse has become the norm. And of course, from the perspective of shareholders, customers are being happily engaged in delivering the business plan. They are keeping planes in the air, helping reduce costs, and simultaneously improving service.

5. Love Bomb

How did the Moonies (more correctly, members of the Unification Church) seduce recruits at their famous weekends? They employed a technique that came to be called "love-bombing." Love-bombing consisted of a continuous, often exhausting series of exercises that made the potential recruit feel that they belonged to the happiest, most welcome group they had ever tripped over. It was an environment where all judgement was suspended and criticism banned.[4]

The Moonies were in a sense "hot-housing" the same technique the Mormons use in recruitment. They were making fast-sealing bonds of attachment between the visitors and the cult by forcing the lines of social interaction with their community. The ideology of the cult, new and strange as it was to many, was cushioned within the comfort of unconditional love. The technique formed social bonds, especially to those already in the cult, so that "Final conversion was coming to accept the opinion of one's [new] friends."[5] The power of overwhelming welcome was the Moonie's prime recruitment methodology.

Mary Kay love bombs on a scale that would make the Moonies green with envy. It also has significantly more members than the Unification Church has ever enjoyed. Of course, many consider Mary Kay a full-blown cult, or at least a relatively harmless and somewhat amusing one, and assume its perky members are victims of the transfixing voodoo typical of such manipulative organizations. However, the reality is more sensible than sensational. The strategy for recruitment of both sales consultants and customers (many of whom become sales consultants) is to coddle the prospect, to support and love them, to make them feel they are the most important people on earth. The consultants I spoke to were quite adamant that they will never go into a selling situation and sell. The rhetoric they used eschewed this concept entirely. Instead they will present themselves as a catalyst for a party, or, if one on one, the handmaiden to the transformation of a women into her more confident self. They consider that it is the relationships that are formed and the attention fostered that make the sale, not a naked pitch.

Business and religion alike have overlooked the *power of the person*. The currency of the term "cult of the individual" is an indication of the value given by our society to self-determinism. In other words, decisions are considered to be made on the basis of facts, and ideas are believed to be assessed on their merits and not necessarily with reference to others. The assumption that is often made in the marketing of brands and religions is that indeed, all men are islands. The opportunity of utilizing the power of social connections and interaction is frequently missed. However, in the world of conversion, whether to a brand or religion, love conquers all.

Next, we'll look at the power of community and its capacity to influence everything, including the purchase of things and ideas. It examines our undeniable urge to form groups, and the tools that are used to create potent communities. Recognizing the importance of *community* is to accept the effectiveness of the power of the person *multiplied*.

4
YOU BELONG

People live in groups. Every human being enters the world as a member. From the earliest known history, people have lived together in families, clans and tribes, have assembled in neighborhoods, communities, villages, towns and cities and have operated in gangs, clubs, unions, associations, and congregations and innumerable other groups.

The person and the group are not separable phe-nomena, *but are simply the individual and collective aspects of the same thing.*

—Dr. Loren Osborn and Dr. Martin Neumeyer,
Community and Society

The idea of belonging is such an underestimated principle in marketing that I will not only lay out the techniques that allow it to happen, but make the argument why you should bother. Habits are slow to change. The marketing community has only just heaved itself, reluctantly, away from the belief that its consumer is a mass and homogeneous market. It's moved from the broadcast "Yell and Sell" to the extreme opposite point of view—seeing its customers as isolated individuals to whom one conducts "one-to-one marketing." The pendulum has swung too far and entirely missed an insight on how to market effectively.

Marketers should also be engaged in community marketing: cultivating, serving, and infusing brands into communities. Marketers should be obsessed with communities, not just fret about how to market to an impossible number of individuals. This will take a tectonic shift of attitude and practice. Hence, there's a need to outline why it's so important to reorient marketing departments. Because community marketing is going to be the next big thing.

There is one very compelling reason why marketers should focus on developing communities. The human race demands them. In fact, not just demands them, but needs them. Belonging is a fundamental dictate of the human condition. We can't help but want to belong. Not to provide communities is not to satisfy a basic need. And not satisfying a basic need with a commercial answer would be the shame of most business people. It's one that would qualify them to be cast into the business hall of infamy.

We Belong to *Survive*

The great American Myth of Individualism is so pervasive that it requires countering with the more powerful idea of man as a group animal. The rugged frontiersman and heroic entrepreneur are icons of individuality that have informed the driving cultural belief of survival of the fittest. However, those who quote Darwin to prove how elemental solitariness is to the human condition would be dismayed to know that he actually regarded man as an animal whose survival depended on the group. The moment a lone and hungry man with a sharp stick faced a woolly mammoth and realized he needed his friends, human evolution took a lurch forward.

Those who acted in groups stood a better chance of living than those who didn't. And the compulsion to form groups to survive has not gone away, just underground.

Despite the disappearance of woolly mammoths, belonging in social networks still has an impact on man's survival rates, even in our modern and sophisticated society. This has been demonstrated by many studies in the medical world, including an especially vivid piece of research run by Yale University.[1] Researchers documented the social networks, marital status, membership in religious organizations, membership in voluntary groups, friends, and relatives of 194 patients who had been hospitalized by a heart attack. They monitored their recovery rates while making every attempt to isolate other factors from that of social connectedness. The results were dramatic. By the end of the year, 55 percent of those reporting no support had died compared with 27 percent of those with some social network.

Lisa Berkman of the Harvard Public School of Health, one of many medical sociologists and physicians who have studied the effect of social support on cure and recovery rates among their patients, said, "The degree to which we feel a part of our *community* or have deep abiding social and psychological resources help to *determine how protected we are against biological, environmental or interpersonal assaults.*" Deep within our psyche is the need to belong, deep enough for it to have a material effect on our longevity. Evolutionary psychologists would claim that we are genetically programmed as a race to form groups.

We don't just need to belong in order to survive. We also need to belong in order to create a sense of reality and to make meaning—pretty fundamental demands of the human condition.

We Belong in Order to Determine What's *Real*

We belong in order to judge what's real. This seems strange to those of us who have always believed that we individually and intimately interpret the world around us, that we alone decide what's true or false; we perceive the world through the lens of our own personality and form views about how the world works.

Actually, collective agreement on reality strongly influences individual perceptions of what is what. Peter Berger, a renowned sociologist claims, "The subjective reality of the world hangs on the thin thread of conversation."[2] A demonstration that we all make collective agreements on what is real was made in a famous laboratory experiment in the 1930s. The exercise showed the triumph of collective belief over fact and collective will over the individual.[3]

The first stage of the experiment required that individual subjects sit alone in a totally dark room. They were instructed to focus on a single point of light projected onto the wall. The light was shut off and on sporadically. Each research subject was asked to estimate how far the light moved each time that it returned. The light, in fact, did not move. But in the absence of any visual reference points, the light could seem to travel anywhere between an inch and several feet, depending on the individual. And indeed individual estimates varied dramatically.

Participants were then invited to return to the lab in groups of three. Once again, the light was turned off and on sporadically and the group was asked to estimate how far the light had moved. The researcher noted that "As they heard one another's estimates of the light's movement, group members' responses began to converge until they were nearly identical. In coming to this collective opinion or consensus, group members established social norms about the movement of the light." The group's perspective was the most powerful agent in the individual's decision of what was real.

We Belong in Order to Make Meaning

If communities help us create a sense of reality, then they can be even more depended upon to interpret the metaphysical. Peter Berger also created the notion of "plausibility structures"—social constructs that support agreement on the most intangible and yet the most important issues of life beyond survival: what it all *means*. In the face of terrifying chaos and the cruelty of randomness, humankind has a craving need to make sense of it all and to create order. It is through the agency of the group that meaning is made, each member reinforcing the believability of an interpretation to the other, each institution asserting the plausibility of its belief system by the evidence of the collective buy-in of its membership.

A. Marie Cornwall, the sociologist who conducted the study on the effect of the group on belief and commitment, said the following: "Individuals come to adopt a particular worldview through some form of socialization . . . their religious worldview is sustained by conversations with others who are also religious." She found in her exhaustive quantitative study that both the strength and frequency of "in group ties" (those within the Church versus those outside) "have the strongest influence on belief and commitment." In other words, there is a high correlation *between belonging to a group and belief in its worldview.*

All of this is not to say that the notion of the individual is irrelevant or unimportant. But it is an attempt to reassert the role and importance of community. Moreover, as we saw in chapter 1, I'm also asserting that a community is actually instrumental in the development of the individual. Far from denying individuality, community enables it. "Belonging makes me more me" according to a cult member I interviewed. This paradox was consistently confirmed whether I talked to members of a cult, social group, or brand community, whether Krishna, Marine, sorority, Trekkie, or Apple addict.

But aren't communities dying? Politicians, the media, church leaders, and the chattering classes are all ruing the loss of community and blaming most social ills on its disappearance. The modern age of tract housing with no definable borders and the increased mobility of Americans who move location on an average of every seven years are all putting pressure on our notions of community. The stressed out, profoundly tired, time-starved average American simply hasn't got time to join anything. Indeed, research figures confirm the typical person's desire to be involved in the community has increased as their opportunity to do so has decreased. In 2002, 65 percent of Americans see more and more of an advantage in being part of a community.[4]

"Community" Has *not Disappeared*

Community has not gone away. It cannot because it's too fundamental to the human condition. It's just changed its appearance. Like any successful organism that survives a change, it has evolved. And it has evolved in a way that lends itself to brands becoming a locus of belonging. The time has arrived for brands to take their place among others as new iterations of community in contemporary society.

Robert Wuthnow in his book *Loose Connections* documents how the new shapes of social interaction are less formal, demand shorter periods of commitment, and are more focused on specific goals in response to the new demands of modern citizens. For example, traditional social groupings such as the Elks and Rotary Clubs are experiencing a decline in attendance and membership. This is not necessarily because there are fewer businesses or that people want to network less, or that they have less of a social conscience. But it is because people have less time to spare, are relocating more often, and if they have time available do not wish to commit themselves to organizations that have large obscure objectives with significant time commitment. Belonging to a group that works to build a new gym for the school or protest the building of a local power plant is more likely to get a membership than the older institutions that had officers and lifetime memberships and sought to remedy everything from poverty to litter. Wuthnow argues that Americans are "experimenting with looser, more sporadic ad hoc connections in place of the long term memberships in hierarchical organizations of the past."[5]

As the railways, highways, airways, telephone, mass media, and the Internet erode the concept of the traditional community, they also create new ones. Unanchored and imagined communities of others that share a state of mind rather than physical proximity have joined the geographic neighborhood. Gradually, a businessman in Columbus, Ohio, has realized that he shares, and feels more strongly, a community of interest with other businessmen and women in San Francisco, or New York, or São Paulo rather than with his neighbor down the street who fixes cars.

As the nostalgic icons of community (the bucolic images of rural small towns, Main streets, and garden fences where physical proximity enabled people to interact) has slipped away, they've been replaced by communities of ideas and mutual interest. And the electronic age has enabled this evolution in ways that few imagined even a few decades ago. Political leaders can extend their "church" and gather funds on the Internet rather than door-to-door. Groups of collectors can meet on eBay rather than travel to exhibition halls. Friendster has catapulted friendship, dating, and straightforward networking beyond anything that was possible when the world was trapped by traditional geographically based contact.

Brands Are Becoming Legitimate Centers of Community

Into this reformation of community slips the notion of brand community. Mediated by modern forms of communication, brand communities have become a modern belonging phenomena, appropriate to contemporary demands. They can be ideological. They can provide venues for social interactivity that demand lower levels of commitment than their parents or grandparents felt compelled to when they subscribed to the traditional forms of social interaction. They may not fulfill the demands created by nostalgic notions of community (although some do), but they can and do provide venues for association that are more relevant to contemporary conditions.

A recent study of brand communities by Albert Muniz and Thomas O'Guinn found that specialized, non–geographically bound communities of admirers are gathering around brands.[6] They found that communities that had formed around the Ford Bronco, Saab, and Macintosh computer brands exhibited all the traditional markers of sociologically defined groups. These minisocieties, which supercede traditional communal boundaries of county, state, and nation, all foster an intrinsic sense of connection between their members and a collective sense of difference from those not within the community. They all have conventions, rituals, and traditions that set up visible public definitions. And they exhibit a sense of obligation on the part of members to the community as a whole and to other individuals in the group.

Perhaps you're feeling a little superior at the moment. *You* don't belong to a brand community. Your commitment to a brand would never go to those absurd lengths. You just buy brands for their use-value. Yet don't deny that you've looked at the driver of the same model of car as yours when you've pulled alongside them at a stop-light. Haven't you felt indignant if they are not like you? You might take one look at them and decide that they should forfeit their car immediately at the nearest dealership. And if they are like you, you might offer a slight nod of recognition. In other words you've imagined that owners of that brand should be like you, share your interests, that you'd probably get along if you met at a party. In other words, you are part of an "imagined community."

It is impossible not to notice a palpable sense of community around the Apple brand. There is a commonwealth of people who feel complicit with each other whenever they see the Mac icon. I sometimes go to a café near my office to escape the hurly burly and have space to think. It's the kind of place where you can mull over a cup of coffee and be left undisturbed for hours while you contem-plate big issues or problems in your work. Most people are writing and reading. The clientele tend to be professional writers, profes-sors, and some journalists, and we all use Macs. We never mention it because it's kind of a given. This unspoken brand community be-comes even more apparent if someone walks in with a PC. There is an observable shiver throughout the room, almost like the moment when Tom wore the wrong clothes at the Harley bar. This person does not belong, what are they doing here? Being polite we say nothing but there must be a discernable sense of groupness, and its partner, exclusion, because these benighted individuals never come back. Since I bought my Titanium G4, the people who dash in for a take-out coffee have looked at my laptop on the way out, looked up at me, and nodded with a smile.

Forty-five thousand Saturn owners and their cars turned up at the Saturn plant—in Tennessee. They were average people from all over America who, when others might have gone to Disney-world, Yellowstone, or the Grand Canyon for their vacation that year, brought their families instead to a car plant—in Tennessee. Why? Why would their kids let them? Because they wanted to meet the people who made their car, and the makers wanted to meet them. They wanted to meet other Saturn owners and their families. Saturn retailers wanted to meet other retailers, other customers, and rekindle relationships with friends at the plant. They all wanted to share barbecue together, listen to some country music and rock and roll, play sports, and have their pictures taken with other owners.

Saturns are well made but otherwise very ordinary cars. A nerdy and obsessive interest in the cunningly crafted carburetor (to be honest, I don't know whether it is or not, but I suspect not) was not the reason for these people to get together. The car had become the locus for one of the largest brand communities the country has ever seen. The "Homecoming" as it was called, was the first of many events that brought that community together in a traditional form. It was an old-fashioned tent meeting for a new kind of religion.

The Homecoming took place three years after the brand was launched. By that time the cult was thriving, having used a mixture of traditional and modern community-building tools. It used both bricks and mortar in the form of its dealerships and media to create real and virtual town halls for the group. It united millions of people with a common belief system and sense of mutual interest that transcended barriers of geography and background. And it used actual and surrogate contact between members to create a sense of belonging. The Saturn phenomenon is one example of many brand communities that have eclipsed many traditional forms of connectedness.

Let's look now at how this was done by also comparing it and other cult brands with some more traditional communities. Whether car-focused or god-focused, these groups have been built with tools that have forever stimulated the age-old desire to belong and have used the same perennial techniques for creating communities.

5

CULTING IS A CONTACT SPORT

The more cult members are around each other, the stickier the bond. Interaction, contact, and frequent engagement between members are the surest means to develop unbreakable connections to each other, to the group as a whole, and to its doctrine.

The Mormon Church has over eleven million members in 162 countries. Size, rapid growth, and huge geographic spread are normally the death of committed and cohesive communities. Yet the church has reconciled the mutually exclusive. Smaller commercial or religious organizations that cover less territory should be jealous of its achievement.

How has it done it? It has a very impressive contact strategy and program. As we examine its strategies in this and subsequent chapters we'll look at the church as if it were also a corporation with eleven million devoted employees (several leading pundits and publications have claimed as much) or a worldwide brand with eleven million loyal customers. Could you also grow a brand to leadership status while maintaining such intense consumer loyalty?

A. Marie Cornwall's study of the Mormon Church found that the greater the degree of interaction among members and the larger the number of relationships within the church, the more the individual's behavior showed signs of commitment (as indicated by their adherence to the cult's doctrine).

Indeed, Latter-day Saints are more involved than members of other large churches. They express a stronger affiliation with the church,[1] and they also contribute more annually (Mormon men—$1,846, Mormon women—$1,562 versus the U.S. average: men—$421, and women—$403). The originators of this data claim "there are substantial differences between Latter-day Saints and other Americans. Latter-day Saints people are more likely to be highly religious, to believe oneself to be a strong member of one's church, to believe in life after death, and to make greater financial contributions to the church."[2]

My own interviews confirmed an extraordinary commitment and revealed what appeared to me an arduous amount of energy devoted to the church given modern demands on time. Most of that energy was spent engaging with other members.

One such church member, Peggy Fugal, straddles the two worlds of cults and marketing. A feisty businesswoman she is both a Mormon and a marketing expert (she has a successful advertising agency in Salt Lake City). She has made it a personal hobby to look at the church through the lens of her business. She enthused several times during our conversation that "the church is just brilliant at marketing!" She pointed out that its contact strategy is essentially a retention program. It's the glue of the community; it's the source of the cohesion of the group. Fugal, while proud of the success of her own marketing company, is in awe of the church's "marketing savvy" in terms of creating a strong community and member loyalty.

How does the church create this glue? Through a combination of the following three strategies. First, they have established a rigorously applied *program of contact* forcing "high content" engagement between members. They don't just meet at church on Sunday. It's a contact program that occurs during the other six days of the week, and is replicated worldwide. You'll see the same program in force whether you're in Manchester, England, or Manchester, New Hampshire.

Second, they *keep tabs* on their membership and prospects, placing particular focus on recent recruits. They view the latter as those most vulnerable to leaving, knowing that weak contact with existing members will lead to a weakened commitment to the church and its theology as a whole. They use the membership at the local level as informants to feed and monitor the database. They collate information for a local, regional, national, and international database where it is interrogated at every stage to check on the members' location and degree of involvement. Third, *the membership runs the program themselves,* with direction from the cult leaders. It's contact by the people for the people. This creates a high degree of involvement in the community and a sense of responsibility among members for the welfare of each other and the group as a whole.

The Contact Strategy

Like that other successful religion that grew fast with a devoted membership in its first three hundred years, Christianity, the Mormon Church has institutionalized a rigorous program of contact that caters to both members' temporal and spiritual needs. Followers really have no need to call on anyone but the church for its secular or spiritual demands. It has created a self-sufficient world of contact and care.

Home visits take place a minimum of every four weeks. They are conducted by the males of the church who "bear the priesthood" (normally acquired at the age of twelve by men only). The purpose is to "visit members regularly, showing love for them, teaching them the gospel, and inviting them to come unto Christ.

Home teachers should encourage fathers to pray and take proper care of their families. Home teachers help members in times of illness, loss, loneliness, unemployment, and at times of other special needs."[3] They normally discuss the "First Presidency Message" (a doctrinal lesson issued by the leadership once a month) with the family or individual.

The women's organization, known as the Relief Society, is dedicated to providing welfare to members. This can range from meeting fellow ward members' families at the airport to cooking and delivering meals during periods of sickness. The 10 percent tithe goes to the building of chapels and temples, but it also helps finance this and other care programs. Peggy Fugal says, "There isn't a Mormon on the planet on welfare." Women fulfill the role of "Visit Teaching," which also takes place a minimum of every four weeks. Two "sisters" visit another sister and deliver a message, and concern themselves with more of the temporal needs of the family or individual. "When you are assigned to be a visiting teacher, an important part of your responsibility is to learn of the spiritual and temporal needs of the sister and her family and to give spiritual instruction through a monthly message. You are a teacher of the gospel."[4]

The family unit is essential and sacred. Every week there is a Family Home Evening, normally on a Monday night. Family bonding is institutionalized on Mondays, with some form of reading or lesson given by the male head of household. When family members are not there, surrogates take their place. Garrett, a young church member in New York, whose family is in Utah, explained "family units among singles."

The night before our interview he had met with friends in a park where "someone shared a message." They then went to McDonald's and ate ice cream. Sometimes they meet at someone's apartment and make cookies. This formalized replication of family interaction can be a very good substitute. He confessed, "I don't feel like I'm far away from my family. In fact, I hate to admit it, but I don't really miss my family when I'm here because I have so many friends who are like my family, you know?" As A. Marie Cornwall claims, the more frequent these moments, the more committed individuals become to the group.

Peggy Fugal, in demonstrating the compassionate, relentless contact strategy, says, "If you're not in church on Sunday, your home teacher is going to notice, your visiting teacher is going to notice, the bishop is going to notice, and somebody's going to call you, and somebody's going to visit with you. And if they discover you're sick, they're going to bring meals in. And if they discover your marriage is in trouble, they're going to find you a counselor. And if they discover you're out of a job, they're going to refer the church employment specialist to you, and get you a job. And if they discover you're out of groceries, they're going to write you a welfare slip to go to the bishop's storehouse to get groceries. This church is brilliant."

Keeping Tabs—Nobody Disappears

The church's membership database is vast, comprehensive, and constantly updated. Its accuracy, currency, and completeness are pursued with unusual energy. Garrett's main function at his ward is "membership clerk." He is one of tens of thousands of worldwide collectors, compilers, updaters, and pursuers who maintain the engine of contact at its most effective level—locally. He saw his role as "fostering communication by making sure that I'm up to date on who's here and who isn't." He maintains an online membership directory that only members of the ward can access. He compiles records of a member's phone numbers, addresses, e-mail, and takes their photographs.

How does he follow the comings and goings of people leaving

the area or arriving, of those who may need help or those who have slipped into nonattendance? Every Sunday after the spiritual meetings of the day, he sits down with the bishop and his attendees and they share information about the members and their needs. This is followed by a Ward Council, which consists of the heads of all of the committees. Grant describes them as his "informants" who tell him who's moved, who's changed their phone number, and who's showing signs of drifting away.

If people have plainly disappeared he'll send a letter to their old address, and if that fails, call their parents to see if they know where their children have gone. He'll then forward the data to the officials of the person's new ward. If the parents don't know where they've moved he sends the data to headquarters "and they try and figure it out."

Fugal proudly points out, "The church never loses track of its members, even if they're totally inactive. They always know where you're living. They always know what ward you're in. They always know who your bishop is. And if you have succeeded in disappearing, they will assign a missionary to find you."

New recruits are also subject to a formal program of contact at the moment that they are most vulnerable to disappearing. Immediately following conversion, the missionaries will keep visiting the individual or family to introduce and teach the church doctrine and its programs of contact, and involve them in those programs. An existing member family is assigned to the recruit to ensure that he or she comes to church, to answer questions and to make sure competitive religions or earthly temptations are not "distracting them from their new choice, their new life." "Brilliant stuff," Fugal continues, "the church knows with a great deal of marketing savvy how to convert and hold onto a convert."

The Members Run the Program

The Church of Latter-day Saints has no paid clergy.[5] Its lay membership fulfills all the obligations of spiritual leadership, teaching, organization, and welfare. The bishops can also be lawyers, doctors, or entrepreneurs by day. A Stake president can own his own restaurant. Apart from freeing up large amounts of the church's income from supporting an otherwise expensive full-time clergy, lay leadership forces intimate involvement between member and institution, and between members and each other. In a sense, the membership runs its own cult.

Ryan, a mergers and acquisition consultant, not only holds down his demanding and stressful job as a senior managing director at his consultancy, but also serves as Stake president. He is responsible for a large number of wards or parishes in a wide geographic area. Within the very clear and multilevel hierarchy of the organization he is responsible for coordinating the spiritual and temporal work with the local managers of each ward. He shares his work with the Stake High Council, which also consists of others in demanding day jobs. "Across the spectrum they are lawyers, doctors, a partner at Deloitte and Touche."

Every member I interviewed, from David Neeleman, the founder and chairman of jetBlue, to young Garrett who's not long out of college, had fulfilled some role in the church normally performed by paid clergy in other organizations. The result? Intimacy with others and the institution. There's a degree of involvement here seldom seen in other organizations, except perhaps in the early Christian church prior to the formation of a priesthood in the fourth century.

The Church of Latter-day Saints is, of course, a religion, and some of its activities are only appropriate to a religious organization.

But not all. Could you not encourage programs of welfare and doctrinal teaching within your organization? Can you involve your consumers in the running of the cult? How good is your database and can your franchise help update it?

How might the Mormons contact strategy be replicated in a commercial context? Isn't it an impossible task to have that much contact and that much "good" data? Most CRM programs (Customer Relationship Management, the direct mail and sales calls to homes, as the general population might better know it) are notoriously inefficient at updating and record keeping and have a relatively low response rate (to achieve upper single digit percentages is cause for celebration).

The key to the Mormons' approach is that first, it is a program *for the membership run by the membership.* It is not corporation to customer, but customer to customer, a big difference. The faceless marketing corporation disturbing your dinner for another few bucks is sidestepped here. It's a fellow member, possibly a friend, disturbing you for something of mutual interest. Second, the *database is run by the membership.* This makes it both current and accurate. Accurate information is more likely to be divulged to a fellow member or worshipper than it is to a corporation. It also is very cheap to run because the members donate their time.

Finally, the nature of the contact is *high content.* The pretext for the frequent engagement between members is to offer something highly valuable—spiritual or temporal. Knowing that someone is always thinking about you and checking on your welfare creates strong emotional bonds. The Mormon visits provide a service, whether to offer something tangible, like hot meals if you are sick, or doctrinal, like a bible reading. Finally, they provide social contact that can simply be fun, like ice cream in the park.

The BMW motorcycle community doesn't think it is a community. Whereas the Harley-Davidson cult members view belonging as a quintessential part of the experience, BMW riders like to think of themselves as the lone wolves of the road. It's their territory and all others are pretenders to its ownership. They are the independent survivalists of the road. They are in it for the experience of the ride, and that's it. Even Harley riders talk about them with respect as the "real riders." As one said, "You just have to look at his odometer to tell he's a BMW rider." These are the guys crazy enough to ride from the icy tip of Alaska to the tip of South America (one rider I spoke with just completed a ten-thousand-mile ride with his son). If BMW riders organize a rally, the point of it is to ride there. Harley riders tend to put their machines on a trailer and offload them in front of the bar to admire each other's impeccably clean chrome over a beer.

But they're kidding themselves. The BMW cult is lesser known than its flashier chrome-bedecked brother, but it is a cult nonetheless. As we'll see, they have their own strong community. Riders have a very acute sense of responsibility toward each other (a critical indicator of the strength of a community) they meet both virtually on Web sites and literally for rides and increasingly at rallies. They have codes of behavior, and an unwritten doctrine. They believe they are different from everyone else, and most believe that they are only truly being whom they are when they are on their machine with other BMW riders. And they have a sense of holier-than-thou often targeted toward the Japanese-manufactured bike-riders.

The BMW cult, like the Mormons, is decentralized. It wants very little to do with the BMW corporation—all it wants is for the company to keep producing high-quality machines. BMW has very smartly respected the independent nature of its clientele. It keeps its distance, and when it does communicate directly with its membership via advertising, its Web site, sales materials, and mail shots it's done in the tone and manner of rider-to-rider, not corporation to rider. Everything is written as if one gritty warrior of the road is talking to another, and often they are. Most of the marketers and personnel on the account at the advertising agency are BMW riders themselves and are equally obsessed with the experience.

The equivalent of the Mormon contact strategy in this decentralized cult is executed though the BMW MOA (Motorcycle Owners Association). It's an organization numbering 35,000 members and is run totally independent from the corporation (independent but not hostile). It describes its aim as "communication based on mutual sharing of ideas, talents, concepts and experiences, so the knowledge and enjoyment of our sport will substantially increase through *collective education and participation.*" That last phrase (my emphasis) could describe the Mormon contact strategy. It has elected officers who are drawn from the general population of rider-members.

How do they execute their stated objective? They have a highly effective database of members "recruited through the Web site, from other members, and from the dealers and local chapters," said an MOA spokesman. It's run by the membership, informed by the membership and local "churches," and information is compiled at a central point. "Welfare" and instruction is given by local chapters who meet each month and the national yearly rally where there is a "family atmosphere" as the spokesperson described it. Seminars are given by volunteers on a whole range of issues from technical problems to the best and most stimulating rides. The only paid staff are the office workers.

The MOA is one of several rider organizations that operate with similar contact strategies and have a similar sense of rider ownership of the community and involvement in running it. For example, the IBMWR (International BMW Rider Association) refers to all members as presidents in recognition that they "own" the brand. There are two publications that are published by rider communities (the OTL—*On The Level,* and *BMW ON*).

What if you want more direct involvement in the contact strategy of your cult or brand community? Supposing you don't want to leave it entirely to the membership. Don Hudler, ex-CEO of Saturn and now the owner of six Saturn retail outlets in Texas, was one of the instigators of many of the famous community building and contact creating strategies at the car company.

The Saturn community was a Holy Trinity. The manufacturers, whether management or line workers, the retailers, and the customers saw no division between each other in their commitment to the brand, to each other, and to the brand community of Saturn as a whole. With that in mind the nature of the contact included all three elements of the Trinity from the start.

Every month most Saturn dealers hold car clinics to explain the fundamentals of maintenance and basic emergency procedures like changing a tire. These typically take place on an evening and the retailer will provide entertainment and a barbecue. The invitations are made within thirty to ninety days of the purchase of the car (like the Mormons, creating contact with recent recruits) or their last attendance at an event. The response rate is high: typically between 35 to 50 percent. These events "reinforce the decision the customer has made for our brand, and maintains a relationship over their lifetime." And it is a relationship that has depth. These events involve everyone in the retail outlet from receptionist to technicians to sales consultants, not just the customer relationship people. Everyone manages the relationship, and all are part of the community.

This is an example of a high-content form of contact. The customers are receiving practical information, food, entertainment, and even friendship between customers and between customers and employees. One of the high-content moments enjoyed by customers is when their car is raised up on the lift and the technicians point out things that they need to know. This breaks down the age-old wariness of mechanics by demystifying the car and building trust.

Other scheduled contact is made by phoning the customer after every form of engagement with the retailer—service, repair, purchase, or recall—and checking if everything is satisfactory. If a recall is necessary, it's turned from a potentially negative blemish on the brand into another opportunity for contact. The dealer hosts a barbecue, gift certificates might be handed out for local restaurants, and the personnel at the retailer are on hand to answer questions and generally reassure the customer.

One centrally organized and locally applied activity to create contact was the construction of playgrounds in local neighborhoods. Members of the Saturn plant—often the people who built the cars—the local retailers and customers donated their time to build playgrounds in impoverished areas with financing made available by the company. It represented a high contact and highly rewarding content-based interaction among all members of the Trinity. Over a hundred playgrounds were built across the country at between $50,000 to $100,000 each.

The retailers will often undertake contact activities that might otherwise be run by owner's groups. They will invite drivers on rallies around the countryside, sometimes 100- to 150-mile trips with refreshments and entertainment. Saturn hosts days at theme parks. For example, a regional group of retailers will take over a Six Flags Park for the day and invite owners to play and socialize together. At one organized at Carrowinds near Charlotte, North Carolina, last year, Hudler reported that approximately ten thousand customers turned up.

At the first Homecoming event customers traveled from as far as Alaska and Taiwan. Others caravaned from the West Coast. Winona Judd performed, there was face painting, and washable Saturn tattoos were handed out. The most popular event according to Don was a tour of the plant. When he first suggested it the line workers were concerned that it would reduce productivity by slowing the line down (not a concern often heard by the average car worker—an indication of the sense of responsibility felt toward the community of the brand). In fact, they set a productivity record each of the two days of the event. The owners took pictures of the makers of their cars; the makers took pictures of the owners. The line workers made banners and kids helped them.

Whether your organization participates overtly in the contact program or distances itself from one that already exists and is run by the membership, there must be one for the community to be robust. The Mormon organization does both. Its program (and the Church) is centrally controlled from Salt Lake City via an extremely well-defined hierarchy and a legislated program of contact, but the members run it themselves. Both the content and the database is conducted and furnished by those who benefit from it.

The BMW corporation is also becoming more involved with the membership community. But it's doing it in a fashion that renders it acceptable to a fiercely independent population. Real everyday riders give the seminars it sponsors with a few guest appearances by celebrated designers and other notables within the corporation. All of its advertising and communications feature real riders who then also appear at these events to give instruction and advice. The language and subject matter of the communication betray an intimate knowledge of what it is like to be a real rider (in fact that is the communication strategy: "BMW is the indisputable mark of the real rider"). In short, it is supporting and sponsoring an existing brand community and not blundering in and attempting to control it. It recognizes that the cult has its own very effective program of contact and its role is nurturer not controller. The last thing that Lawrence Kuyrendall wants to do is upset "the tight-knit group" that he has working for him, albeit remotely, as a community builder.

6

WE'RE IN THIS TOGETHER

C ult members must engage with each other, that we know. Now what must happen for bonds to become unbreakably strong? There are two critical and related characteristics of cohesive communities: shared experience between members, and a sense of responsibility and mutual dependence. Strong communities develop as intimacy between members grows. The membership must share experiences, remember them together, compare their interpretations, and tell stories about them. Strong bonds are created once members feel an obligation to each other and the group as a whole. That members have a sense of mutual dependence is perhaps the clearest indicator that their community is becoming a cult.

Shared Experience

Being in the same school, town, generation, country, or era forms attachments based on common experience and shared meaning. Shared experience is vital to the cohesion of a cult. In fact, cults are the masters of creating community based on mutual experience and the collective memory of that experience. Let's look at a cult where shared experience is hothoused amongst its members. It is the kind of experience created by close contact and defined by immediacy.

Mike, a young, recently graduated second lieutenant in the Marines, dared me to call him a cult member. It didn't take too long to convince him it was true. He could not deny that his calling had all of the classic characteristics of a radical belonging organization. It had a clear and rigorously applied ideology. It had rules and regulations, ritual, traditions, mythology and storytelling, hierarchies, an acute sense of difference from the world around it, and an unashamed sense of moral superiority. He agreed that he had "become himself" to a degree which civilian life could never provide, and that it had happened through the agency of a brotherhood like no other. There was uniformity of appearance and language. There were common symbols and potent iconography. There were enemies, both actual and internalized (such as fear of failure).

I interviewed two second lieutenants, a graduate (Mike) and another still in training (Jon). I also talked to an old salty ex-Marine (Steve, who will be furious at this description. He claims, as they all do, that "there are no ex-Marines, just old Marines"). And I interviewed retired Lieutenant General Martin Steele on an aircraft carrier in New York harbor. His new job is running the Sea-Air-Space Museum on the *Intrepid*. Both elder Marines served in Vietnam and the two lieutenants have subsequently served in Iraq.

Martin Steele claimed that, "We don't care about you as an individual," words he'd said in reference to a recruit's identity when they crossed the threshold of the training camp. In truth, his stories betrayed a profound concern for those individuals for whom he had been responsible.

The induction process is a "breaking down and building up experience." It is one that crystallizes the individual through a group experience. They are rigorously trained physically and in the craft of their job over a twelve-week period. And the single most important idea branded into them over that intense period is that they are totally dependent on the group for their survival. The climactic event over the three month ordeal is called "the Crucible." By then any baggage from civilian world outside has been atomized and any doubts about their own personal ability and the rightness of the institution's ideas have been eradicated. As Jon said, "It's good because there is no doubt about anything."

By the time you reach the Crucible, Steele said you've "got an aura of self-confidence . . . you have been transformed, you believe you are somebody." He stressed that these recruits' sense of self— far from being eliminated by the process—had been developed and enhanced the moment the recruit crossed the threshold. But, the whole point of the training and this ultimate exercise was to "realize that you have very little capability unless you become part of this team," a principle at the heart of the Marine culture.

The Crucible is daunting. It is a grueling event where the recruit is wakened in the middle of the night by a cacophony of noise and screamed orders. The purpose is to instill disorientation and confusion into the group. The recruits are marched into the night to an unknown destination, separated from their normal unit, and assigned to another, much in the way they would replace a casualty in the course of a battle. It's forty hours of no sleep, no food, and long hauls on foot with full kit.

The event takes place on Parris Island, South Carolina, and outside San Diego. Steele described the Crucible's emotional climax, when six hundred recruits come down the mountain in California with the sun at their back and the ocean at their front. As the recruits approached "For the first time the senior enlisted Marine calls them 'Marine,' and the recruit cries and all the drill instructors cry."

The Crucible is a rite of passage by which an individual is transformed through the agency of a shared experience. Steele makes this point by recalling a young man who had been a wrestler at the

University of Michigan. He was "extremely strong, he probably had a twenty-one- or twenty-two-inch neck and fifty-five- or fifty-six-inch chest. He was just a mammoth man of tremendous strength." Steele watched as "tears were running down his muddy face when they handed him our emblem, the eagle, globe, and anchor." He went up to the new Marine after the ceremony and asked why the former champion wrestler had cried. He asked what's the difference between being a wrestler at the top of your league and going through this experience. The new Marine replied, "As a wrestler, it's one-to-one. I'm now part of an organization for eternity. And it's so different. Did I have more physically demanding things in the wrestling room at Michigan? Generally, I did. But I never had anything where I had to be part of a team. And you can never take this away from me."

The Marines, of course, are an example of perhaps the strongest shared experience community in the world. As Steele puts it, "It's a team that transcends sports teams and the civilian community to this life team. Because the business . . . in this elite organization is life and death. It's not a touchdown or a home run. It totally transcends all of that."

Jon, the recent officer recruit, gave his perspective on how that bond is created. Being in lockstep with your compatriots at every single moment "brought everyone together. It kept everyone on the same page. And your sense of collective unity was enhanced that much more. Everyone goes through the exact same thing and I can't underscore enough that everyone is dealing with the exact same problem you are dealing with. You are dealing with it together. You're put in that situation of chaos and everyone knows what you're going through."

Experience can be shared literally, as in the case of the Marines. And it can be experienced metaphorically. The WWF brand (World Wrestling Federation) offers more of the latter to its membership. I interviewed two friends who had met at a bar where the patrons watched the latest episode. They were in their mid-to-late twenties. Kevin handled East Coast sales for a press clipping agency and Gary was a PR consultant. Their choice of careers is relevant. Their jobs are in the media, they know about the art of storytelling, and they know how well emotions can be manipulated with an artful narrative. They're part of the so-called media machine.

They happily admit that they are the willing victims of skillful storytelling by the WWF. They confessed that this sport "is not a sport, it's a masculine ballet. Everything is orchestrated and well choreographed." It's a "good Hollywood movie," Kevin admitted, and they were totally engrossed. They both have had to defend their obsession in the face of derision from colleagues and friends who saw it as a juvenile drama that duped a gullible audience. Kevin and Gary were at pains to prove that they knew it was all fabrication, "that they have script-writers," and that it was just "wholesome entertainment, just entertainment."

But was it? As Kevin later confessed in the interview, "It's strange too, because I'm actually noticing a disconnect in what I've been saying today." He explained that while he enjoyed the fantasy of the weekly dramas, he had also just "highlighted my love of the realism of it, which is strange to me."

What could be realistic about a pantheon of cartoonlike characters that perform weekly to scripts with plot lines that they both described as "preposterous"? During the course of the interview it became apparent that the two men were bonded to others in the bar, and to millions in their homes across the nation, by the dramatization of a Master Narrative. That is, they were all watching a drama that spoke to millions, which referenced the common experience of average men and women.

The identification with the characters and the story lines, as preposterous as they might be, was intense. Kevin gave The Rock as an example: "he's a wise guy, and I consider myself to be a wise guy, almost to a fault as my boss will attest." He admitted that he saw himself in The Rock in "vivid Technicolor . . . I have the feeling that the guy who plays the character of The Rock is probably just like me and he just takes it to the next level." I asked him if he would like to take it to the next level in real life: "In my dream world, but in the real world you just can't . . . you can't speak to people that way. There are ramifications to it."

It was evident that these were dramas in which everyone's proxy played out their daily dilemmas and concerns, and like every good story, the bad guys got their just desserts. The story line at the time was Stone Cold Steve Austin versus Vince McMahon, the president of the WWF. Real life was part of the drama. Vince has been induced to wet himself onstage to demonstrate his fear of his own employees, and he has suffered being hit with a bedpan. Gary believed that what he saw on screen was a universal story. Every week the stories include "people who are hurting their boss, smacking their boss around" and it's, he confessed, "everything every man in America would love to do, and they [the characters] get to do it every week, and they get the crowd cheering for it."

Gary described the brand as a never-ending story of "revenge and redemption." It was reduced to good versus evil. Of the evil guys, Kevin revealed that "we got them" in the office and that "I don't want to deal with them any more." Instead he lets "Kurt Angle handle it in the ring. And I know it seems silly, but on a subconscious level it kind of helps out a little bit."

The WWF brand cult creates shared experience by storytelling. It dramatizes stories that millions share and relate to their own personal narratives. It speaks to their own dialogues they have with themselves about how the world works, what people are like, what they as individuals are like, and where they fit in the order of things. And it is played out profitably to the satisfaction of millions of average Americans, even to cynical media manipulators like Kevin and Gary. It has cleverly picked the shared experience of a majority and co-opted it as its brand content.

Storytelling is a classic form of experience sharing. And it is not limited to brands that make it their product benefit. At jetBlue, mythologies have a currency among staff and customers alike as ways of creating common meaning. Steve Jobs is a story creator for a company that sells boxes of electronics. His master story of iconoclast who became rich and changed the world is a narrative vicariously shared by the millions. It is the classic American Dream. A mass finger at faceless monopolistic empire builders is what most ticket buyers are gesturing, to some degree, when they fly on Virgin.

A Saturn buyer I talked to bought the brand in part because it was a statement from a little guy to abusive car manufacturers: the small, timid car buyers can be treated with respect. A VW Beetle driver I interviewed (he had owned six in succession since his student days in the sixties) admitted that he was buying into the collective story of rejection of materialist values every time he bought one of those "rickety little cars and flashed my headlights at other owners who felt the same way as we passed each other."

Group events offer another opportunity for members to share experience. Followers can exchange stories, testify, hear sermons from the leaders, make friends, and establish networks of support. Organizations employ them to create a sense of solidarity through mass action. Wal-Mart starts every morning with a group cheer; Mary Kay has a mammoth annual meeting in Dallas that is almost evangelistic; Macworld draws thousands of the faithful every year; owners clubs, from Miata to Harley, organize rallies where people share stories, food, and ride together.

We Look after Each Other

A sure indicator of a cult's vigor is the strength of the sense of responsibility that exists within it. Do cult members feel a personal concern for the welfare of their compatriots? Do they look after each other in times of duress? Will they train, financially support, and morally sustain each other? As well as looking out for each other, members should also have a sense of personal investment in the fortunes of the cult itself. Will they make sacrifices to ensure its well being? And critically important is whether the cult feels an equal sense of responsibility toward its members. Is their investment reciprocated? This mutuality is the defining doctrine of any strong culture.

Mutual responsibility is, of course, an *outcome* of the sense of belonging that exists within the group. It's generally an indicator of the cohesiveness of the cult. The stronger the sense of mutual responsibility, the stronger the cult. And the more successfully the programs that have been put in place to create a sense of belonging, the more likely will you see a strong sense of mutuality.

But you can also predispose a culture towards mutuality, even legislate for it. Responsibility can be embedded as an idea within the cult's doctrine and its codes of behavior. This is something to be seriously considered. Mutualism is both a great bonding device and growth strategy. Encouraging your cult toward it is likely to yield the often unreconcileable benefits of growth and loyalty.

Let's look at two cults, one religious and one military, that have codified mutual responsibility with dramatic effect. Then we'll look at two brand cults, one with a centrally militated doctrine of care, the other with an unwritten code that emerged spontaneously from its membership without any involvement from the center.

Christianity might have remained one of many minor cults in the Eastern Mediterranean in the first three centuries had it not been for two devastating plagues and its doctrine of mutualism. In 165 A.D. and again in 251 A.D. plagues of similar ferocity and lethalness as those in medieval Europe spread across the Empire, scything down between a quarter and a third of the population. By that time, Rodney Stark in *The Rise of Christianity* asserts, the Christian values of "love and charity had . . . been translated into the norms of social service and community solidarity. When disaster struck, Christians were better able to cope because of their doctrine of mutual love and care, and this resulted in *substantially higher rates of survival.*"

Modern medical experts, according to Stark, have calculated that conscientious nursing care, without any medications, could cut mortality rates by two-thirds or more. And ministering to the sick is what the Christians did, staying in the cities, looking after their own and other communities. In contrast, their pagan neighbors' routine response to such calamities was to abandon their families and friends and flee. Dionysus, Bishop of Alexandria, noted that ". . . they pushed the sufferers away and fled from their dearest, throwing them into the roads before they were dead and treated unburied corpses as dirt."

The ratio of Christians to pagans after the two plagues dramatically increased. Prior to the first, Stark estimates that the Empire's Christian population was approximately 0.4 percent. Following the second, he estimates the ratio had ballooned to be roughly one Christian to four pagans.[1] Now the religion had become a major influence in the Empire. Contributing to its status was of course what could only have been interpreted as a miraculous survival rate amongst Christians. But even more important to the religion's subsequent dominance was the greatly increased number of social bonds between Christian and heathen. Remembering the effect of "the power of the person" in conversion, interaction between the pagan who replaced his or her friends and family with Christian members had now greatly increased. Survival rates, evidence of the benefits of mutuality within the cult, and the increased social routes for conversion all contributed to the acceleration of Christianity from minor cult to state religion.

The Marines are famous for the cohesiveness of their units, too. They're also famous for their fiercely upheld and self-defining idea of "never leave a fellow Marine behind." In basic training, for example: "We have a ritual in the Marine Corps early on that if a person falls out of a run, you just circle until the guy captures his wind, and he becomes ready to go back in. They don't leave him behind," Mike told me. This is seared into every recruit so that it becomes a reflexive action. It has to be because it's a matter of life or death. Knowing that your fellow members will always come back for you spurs members to greater feats. "In combat, we are notoriously famous for never leaving a Marine on the battlefield. We are the only service that does that. Others say they do, but they don't. But we will do whatever it takes to go back and carry our wounded and dead off of a battlefield. That ethos, if you will, is bred in you from the outset," as Martin Steele told me.

It's in the little things that this code is institutionalized. Jon, another marine, echoed what Steele said: "He's your brother [any other Marine]. And the first few weeks show you that more than anything else. You have to work as a team. If you are done with your gear, every candidate—if he's worth anything—would say 'I'm done, who needs help?'" Both of these examples demonstrate the power of codified mutual responsibility as a community builder and, in the case of Christianity, growth strategy.

Mutuality has been codified in the brand world too. A sales organization is normally one that breeds competition and a culture of dog-eat-dog. Especially if it is based on commission. And direct sales companies (the Amways and Avons of this world) are normally characterized by relentless, hardened, and competitive salespeople. Not so at Mary Kay. The culture of support and "praise," as the founder put it, is driven by her founding principle of giving women the confidence and opportunity to reach their potential, which they don't find in the male-dominated world of business (even nowadays). The binding group culture unified against the hostile world out there fosters a compassion and ethos of support between sales consultants rarely seen in other sales organizations (not even at the highly principled P&G where I was a sales representative for a while).

This is manifested in the doctrine handed down by the founder Mary Kay in the "Mary Kay Values." "Then and now, everything anyone in our sales organization does to succeed is based upon helping others. As beauty consultants we must help customers; and as sales directors we must help our people to succeed. The company structure requires each person to help others in order to climb the ladder of success. The individual who thinks, 'What's in it for me?' will never make it in our company. We truly believe that if you help enough other people get what *they* want—you will get what *you* want! The people who are the most successful in our company are those who have helped the most people grow."[2]

The mantra that "Teamwork allows each person to be valued and appreciated by others" is palpably felt at such events as the Dallas Seminar, where consultants come together to celebrate one another's achievements. The sense of mutual responsibility is manifested not just in the seminars run by consultants that teach skills, but in one to one counseling that happens in the bars and over coffee breaks between enthusiastic members.

BMW bikers have a strong and complex ideology and code of practice. It has spontaneously institutionalized the idea of looking out for the safety of others without any involvement by the corporation. They are gritty, ride-obsessed warriors of the road. But when it comes to the safety of their compatriots, they are as solicitous as nurses. Teddy, a shaved-head, mid-thirties rider in the media business told me: "Riders exchange greetings to each other when they are sitting at that rest stop having a cigarette . . . admiring each other's bike . . . but when they leave they'll all say 'ride safe.' Because they know there's a shared risk." He somewhat guiltily leaves his wife and two young kids and joins a group of BMW riders at six on a Sunday morning for a day ride in the country. (He gets over the guilt quickly, however.) He explained that within this and any group of BMW riders the best would always follow the last rider to ensure that if anyone gets into trouble, someone can take care of him. Much like the Marines. As Teddy said, "You know there's always someone looking out for your back."

One unique manifestation of mutual responsibility is the BMW Owners Anonymous book. It is compiled by the cult membership and updated yearly. It lists the phone numbers of 12,000 riders across America and identifies the help they can give to a stranded, injured, hungry, or lost fellow rider. There are no names beside the numbers, just codes that indicate what kind of support they can offer. If they have a garage for your bike, if they have a pickup truck, if they have an extra room, it will be listed whether you're in Alabama or L.A. As Teddy puts it, "In contrast to the Harley's Owner's Group which essentially takes people on rides, this is an organization that says, 'I know you want to go on a ride, and I want to support you on a ride.' "

Teddy contrasted the feeling he had within this group with his life outside: "It really makes you feel a humanity that you don't get in many areas anymore. It's not charity per se, but you want to help someone, and it's a nice feeling of being connected and being human that I don't get much living in New York City where everyone is competitive."

The BMW Motorcycle cult is an example where the membership created its own culture of reciprocity. The language, the book, the institution of stopping to help another rider when "his helmet is off by the side of the road" was created by the cult members as a manifestation of the bond they felt through a common interest, common values about motorcycling, and a fellowship with others who face the same risks of the road. The BMW Motorcycle cult is a decentralized one, run essentially by the membership. There is a sense that no one on the outside really knows what the pleasures and risks of riding are and therefore only the membership really know what it takes to belong and look after each other.

Mutualism is a crucial ingredient for strong communities. If you can encourage it by legislating for it then do so. EBay has done so within its ideology . . . its business model would fail without the commitment from buyer and seller to honor each other's pledges. Mutualism is the glue of community. Without it the group is fragile. With it the community is bound by common interest and connections rooted in a shared sense of obligation.

7

THIS IS WHAT WE BELIEVE

Because things are so crazy out there, people like to find out if they see the world the same way as other people. People will believe in anything—*from a chocolate bar to a political view—if it makes them feel that they* belong to something bigger than themselves.

—Charlene, loyal Snapple drinker

People today pay for meaning more than they pray for it. In contemporary culture we seek and find answers not only through traditional channels, like religions (and new religions) but also in such places as rock groups, sororities, companies, and brands. If we're managing these kinds of organizations then we have to accept that we're providing venues for making meaning, and that we must therefore devise belief systems, worldviews, and ideologies to enable that fundamental process.

A cult, a company, a brand, a military organization, a fraternity, or a political party must have a meaning system. It's part of what people buy into, a unifying idea structure for the community. It's part of what separates them from others. It's the system that enables members to make sense of the world. And the craving need to make meaning is part of the human condition. And again, if you don't satisfy a craving need with a commercial answer, you should be thrown into the business hall of infamy.

Commercial enterprises need to provide meaning as much as individuals want to buy it. It's a craving need of the commercial world, too. They must produce content beyond the product benefits. Products are cheap, and they increasingly have little or no unique value of their own. Almost every category has been—at least to some degree—commoditized. Many completely. And even if something should flash in the pan—a breakthrough in R&D, an FDA approval that recalibrates the market—it's unlikely it will mean anything for long. As Dave Barger says of the cheap prices, leather seats, and satellite TV on jetBlue planes: "Our competitors will have those in one or two years. It's not what's going to keep people coming back and back again."

Fast-followers circle like vultures on the doorsteps of eureka companies. Product innovations are mimicked almost immediately by the competition, usually cheaper. (Delta's Song is a direct rip-off of jetBlue and launched within three years of the original.) Providing a meaning system that people can buy into is harder to imitate and easier to charge a premium for. No car manufacturer has really matched Mercedes' ability to confer a meaning system of status and achievement to a global audience, despite Lexus and others' best efforts to imitate the products (and sell at a discount). Whether it's good news or not for cultural history, corporations are arguably the most powerful meaning engines today. We spend the majority of our waking hours at work within the confines of a corporate culture. We adopt the language of our business and, often unconsciously, we measure ourselves and our life's value against the values and purposes of the corporate entity that employs us.

The moment we leave the doors of our employers, we walk into a brand-dominated milieu where Diesel Bags flash across the screen on *Queer Eye for the Straight Guy* and Austin Powers ostentatiously drinks from a Heineken bottle. We can't avoid brands. As social scientist Alf Linderman observes in *Rethinking Media, Religion and Culture,* "The mass media [has] become an important site for the development of social meaning, an important point of reference as the individual develops worldviews, and the values embedded in them."

Today's most successful brands don't just provide marks of distinction (identity) for products. Cult brands are beliefs. They have morals—embody values. Cult brands stand up for things. They work hard; fight for what is right. Cult brands supply our modern metaphysics, imbuing the world with significance. We wear their meaning when we buy Benetton. We eat their meaning when we spoon Ben & Jerry's into our mouths. We get inside a company's worldview and fly their meaning when we step onto a Virgin plane, we shop their meaning when we check out at Whole Foods. Driving a Mini is becoming as political as fighting gas-guzzling SUVs via the Sierra Club. Brands function as complete meaning systems. They are venues for the consumer (and employee) to publicly enact a distinctive set of beliefs and values.

If we are going to understand how to make an effective ideology, we should examine why, how, what, and where people make meaning. What are the essential requirements for a functioning belief system that you can apply to your organization?

Let's look at how Anita Roddick of The Body Shop did it. She created a meaning-based brand. Scents, emulsions, and detergents were all things that could be copied (and were). But what she did was build a worldwide empire on a belief system. It was one that millions readily grasped and happily spent billions buying into, from Japan to Jaipur, from Paris to Peoria. (She killed one too, with some equally useful lessons for us to digest on the construction of a meaning-based enterprise.)

BODY SHOP: A MEANING-DRIVEN BRAND

Anita Roddick founded the first Body Shop in the hopes that she would provide just enough revenue to support herself and her two children while her husband was taking a two-year horseback trip from Buenos Aires to New York City. She did. And by tapping into the dynamic of cult brands—by explicitly and consciously providing meaning for her customers—she did a little bit more. At the height of its power in the 1980s, Roddick's Body Shop rose to global conglomerate status—spanning forty-eight countries, at one point, with more than 1,800 outlets in twelve time zones.

How did she do it?

As folklore has it, Roddick "decided to open a small shop in England selling the kind of simple, natural skin and hair care preparations she had seen being used by women of other cultures on her travels around the world."[1] Her patchouli-scented boutique in Brighton, on the south coast of England, opened its dark green interior to longhaired customers in 1976. That dark green continues to color Body Shop retail stores throughout the world—only now it is a top-of-mind attribution cue for a globally recognized brand. Twenty-some odd years ago it was "the only color that would cover the damp patches" in boggy Brighton.[2]

The original Body Shop offered one-stop shopping for a thriving local hippie community. She started with fifteen hand-mixed concoctions, which Roddick packaged in "five different sizes so at least it looked like I had at least 100." Roddick was a hippie herself, an authentic member of an established community. Her business was her passion, a way for her to publicly express her community's values. She wanted her products to mean something, to transcend the canonical messages of beauty and vanity implicit in her competitor's messages.

Roddick brewed up natural concoctions in her garage with "cosmetic ingredients gathered during world treks as a young hippie." Roddick hand-labeled each reusable urine sample bottle, the myth goes, detailing the origin of key ingredients. The Shop's innovative antipackaging gave the raw contents in every vessel an authentic connection to the values of an identifiable meaning system. In a matter of months, peace-lovers throughout Brighton had come to strongly identify with Roddick's eco-friendly free-spirit myths. And the products that carried them. So they kept coming back to refill their bottles with belief and tea-tree soap—at a 15 percent discount for saving the planet.

The next decade was a whirlwind for The Body Shop. A second shop was opened in Chichester within a year of the Brighton shop's premiere. In two years, Anita's husband, Gordon, had structured a franchising scheme to expand the original concept with a minimal capital investment. The first international franchise opened in a Brussels kiosk in 1978. By 1979, Sweden and Greece would be graced with their own Body Shop franchises. "By appointing a head franchisee in each major national market, Roddick was able to concentrate on the development of new product lines and the company's global vision, rather than worry about the complexities of administration or personnel management."[3]

What Roddick was freed up to concentrate on really amounts to one thing not two: The Body Shop's new product lines were completely inseparable from the company's global vision. The product carries the message and then becomes it. From Nepalese paper to Brazilian nut conditioner and all the Indian foot rollers in between, Roddick's personal stories provided the meaning that made The Body Shop, *The* Body Shop. "From the very beginning we wanted to be able to tell stories," Roddick preaches, "We wanted to be honest about the product we sold and the benefits they promised. I . . . see storytelling as a major component of communication within The Body Shop, both stories about products and stories about the organization. Stories about how and where we find ingredients bring meaning to our essentially meaningless products, while stories about the company bind and preserve our history and our sense of common purpose."[4]

And it worked. Roddick created meaning in a category normally condemned as superficial. She practically invented the idea of "natural" in an industry that never imagined the body could be natural, that what you put on it could have significance. "Body Shop products offer an unusual alignment of physical hedonism with spiritual nobility," writes Adam Morgan in *Eating the Big Fish*, "You can sit in your bubble bath and feel as clean inside as you do out. Classically, these two have been opposites: One could either wave placards at a foreign consulate in the driving rain and do the world good, or recline in a scented, foaming bath and do yourself good. Roddick's brilliance has been to reconcile these, to make virtue luxurious, creating an issue brand that requires no social effort on the part of the purchaser except to make the purchase, and then enjoy the effects."[5]

The Body Shop is a meaning-based brand. It encapsulated its core values in what was called The Body Shop Charter, which took eighteen months to complete, because true to its cultural ideology, it involved "grassroots participation in management." It would be as flaccid and useless as most other corporation's values statements if it had remained at that point. Knowing the company was meaning based, that couldn't be allowed to happen, and values were socialized within the organization by "eight working groups . . . to make sure the they penetrated every nook and cranny of the company's operations."[6]

Meaning-based brands make money. Even ones that do not make profit their sole focus (in this Henry Ford agreed with Anita Roddick): "The business of business should not just be about money, it should be about responsibility. It should be about public good, not private greed."[7]

This Is What We Believe

The IPO was red-hot, a legend on London Stock Exchange in 1984, earning BSI (Body Shop International) the nickname "the stock that defies gravity." The ticker displayed 95 pence at first call. It closed at 480 pence, making Anita the fifth wealthiest woman in the United Kingdom in less than a day.[8]

WHAT IS REQUIRED OF A BELIEF SYSTEM?

We'll look at this question through the eyes of Mark who was "definitely searching for something . . . you know, like an answer to life's questions: 'what's it all about? Who am I? Where am I going?' " He is an actor and he felt that he was getting some of all of that from the Landmark Forum's worldview of "get control of your life and take charge of your destiny."

He is a straightforward young man, in his late twenties, dressed in the ubiquitous Dockers pants and an open-necked blue shirt. He's had jobs in the media, finance, and the odd role in plays, very Off-Broadway. From an Italian-American family, he is a no-nonsense, average guy who aspires to the American Dream of a good career, a bit of fame, and personal satisfaction.

There has been an enormous growth of the phenomenon known as Large Group Awareness Training represented by such companies as Landmark Forum. Its former iteration was EST, begun by the famous and infamous Werner Erhard. He retired it in 1985 and started The Forum. One of several cults categorized as examples of the human potential movement that started in the 1970s, it focused on exploring and actualizing the self. It has gained great traction in recent decades with professionals working within highly demanding occupations—entrepreneurs, business managers, the fields of acting, advertising, and marketing. EST and The Landmark Forum have had over a million customers. The latter has forty-three offices worldwide, 420 staff members, and 7,500 volunteers assisting the company.[9] And it has had to defend itself against the suspicion that it is a cultlike organization. Mark said that one of the teachers confessed "Yeah, we're a cult. We're a cult of the most happy people you'll see."

Interpretation, Purpose, and Control

These are the building blocks of a strong meaning system. Interpreting the chaos of the world into some kind of coherent story, creating a goal for one's existence, and a sense of control in the face of the apparent randomness of life are the key roles of a highly functioning meaning system.

Mark's experience as an actor, where the whim of casting agents appeared not just to govern his life, but symbolize on a broader scale all of its frightening unpredictability drove him to find some master story. He needed the structure and order communicated by a coherent doctrine. He needed something that allowed the comforting perception of cause and effect. He wanted something that gave him a larger goal than dealing with the day to day.

The Forum provides its own *interpretation* of how life works, and should work, as any good meaning system should: "People live their lives to avoid repeating or re-experiencing the problems of their past. In doing so, they put their past into their future, and it drives their lives. Our curriculum is designed to allow people to overcome such barriers." A sense of certainty and the *control* that it gives is in the "promise of the Forum." It will "empower you in the face of the risk that life is."[10] Students of these programs are offered conceptual and practical frameworks that claim to channel an individual's energy into a more productive and happier life. Four programs are included in what is called "The Curriculum for Living" (its title has a reassuring ring of order) each at an escalating degree of involvement and cost to the subject.

A colleague of Mark's, also in the program, sought *purpose:* "I believe that life without some other meaning than the day to day routine isn't worth it, or there's just not enough lasting joy and meaning there . . . but I believe there's got to be more and that's what I was looking for." He was expressing a dawning horror of the potential inconsequence of a life lived unconsciously from day to day. According to Mark, The Forum offered purpose. It enabled him to have a more rewarding life by "taking more responsibility over your personal life and future . . . it was kind of empowering."

A cult's, brand's, or any organization's meaning system should also paint a picture of *how the world should be.* It should be aspirational, whether it's a world populated with self-actualized people or one that's ecologically stable.

If we return to The Body Shop for a moment, we can see some of this in Roddick's vision. In a corporate-run world rife with greed and dishonesty, The Body Shop offered customers and employees alike a vision of how things *could be.* The Body Shop's founding interpretive principle was Total Inegrity implemented all the way down the value chain. Honesty and integrity in the way products are sourced, manufactured, marketed, sold, and even consumed. The Body Shop, according to Roddick "is about total honesty . . . the precious First Amendment, the right to publicly debate the performance of any publicly held corporation, and the obligation that we who would measure social costs and benefits have to continue that process, holding ourselves accountable to the standards we set for ourselves."[11]

Roddick's vision gave millions of customers and employees an alternative vocabulary through which to navigate the world. Body Shop employees were not so much salespeople as evangelists spreading their company's purpose. Employees acted as animal-right and hemp activists, as Greenpeace and fair-trade agitators, as community-welfare organizers. Roddick's interpretation of the world allowed customers to feel that purpose with every purchase: support whales, marijuana, a clean ocean, and the third world for a few extra premium cents or dollars with each exchange.

Interpretation, control, and purpose. Satisfy these basic requirements in a worldview for your organization. It should sort and repaint the world into a picture of how it *should* be (one without pollution and exploitation, or without sin, or a society with equality for everyone, or one where being different can change the world).

WHERE DO YOU START?
TWO WAYS TO FIND MEANING

You're faced with the task of creating a belief system for your cult or cult brand. Where do you start? Maybe you are developing a cult from scratch. Perhaps you've inherited one and are dissatisfied with the quality of the system already in place. Where do you begin to find a motivating and satisfying worldview?

It's easier than you think. Some of the work will have already been done for you. Some of the best belief systems, religious or commercial, build on ideas already prevalent in the culture. In fact, there are very few entirely new theologies. Most build on prevailing worldviews, adding some new theology here and there to create enough difference from their surroundings.

Christianity was built upon Judaism; Mormonism was built upon Christianity. Each added their unique ideas to a base of existing culturally acceptable dogma. As such, their ideology was more able to be bought by that culture, but it was different enough to be distinguishable from it.

Another source of an ideology is to take existing beliefs within the community that might have already formed around your brand or cult and simply articulate them (as Harley-Davidson did). We will examine an extremely effective technique used to determine what those beliefs are and how to give them voice. First, some examples of brand cults that took existing cultural beliefs, even subcultural beliefs, and made meaning-driven businesses out of them.

Surf and Steal

The easiest way to get a meaning system for your brand is to tack it onto an existing community's value system. Your brand or cult should become a public symbol for the meaning of this group. They should *feel* that it stands for them. We touched on how Anita Roddick did it for the hippies she lived with in Brighton. She wrote a master story that gave them a voice. Anita found meaning, but didn't invent it.

Ben Cohen and Jerry Greenfield started a "values-led business" (a term they borrowed from Anita Roddick). Their product, ice cream, was packaged with the same kind of political agenda that appealed to the community Roddick found milling around Brighton.

Ben & Jerry's maintained three integral missions: high-quality product, fair profit, and community service. The last of these, serving a community, entails a political agenda—which *targets* a community—the anticorporate left. As such, the milk used to make the ice cream comes from local (Vermont) dairy farms (at a higher price than other milk); the brownies for Chocolate Fudge Brownie were produced by a bakery that trains economically disenfranchised people and reformed criminals; the nuts for Rainforest Crunch come from local Brazilians in an effort to maintain the rainforest via its economic viability.

While Ben & Jerry's ice cream enjoys great loyalty and can demand a premium, it's the political meaning that moves the brand. "Consumers are accustomed to buying products despite how they feel about the companies that sell them. But a values-led company earns the kind of customer loyalty most corporations only dream of—because it appeals to its customers on the basis of more than a product. It offers them a way to connect with kindred spirits, to express their most deeply held values when they spend their money. Unlike most commercial transactions, buying a product from a company you believe in transcends the purchase. Our customers don't like just our ice cream—they like what our company stands for."

As Ben & Jerry's actively promote this meaning, their brand carries these connotations as well. A Peace Pop somehow buys you peace. Where other companies keep their values and politics hidden from consumers, Ben & Jerry's stances are overt. They act as a flagstaff for a uniquely observable community. This strategy, while alienating some, serves to attract many more strongly. Ben and Jerry surfed on existing communities' belief systems and appropriated them. In the process they appropriated the loyalty of those communities.

Observe and Give Voice

Flavored sugar water. Can something as inert and banal as a soft drink have the capacity to carry meaning? Can it create a worldview in which a person can place him or herself and gain a sense of their own identity? Can communities form around such a two-dimensional product? At face value, soft drinks do not have the depth of product interaction and complexity as, say, a motorbike or computer within which such existential needs might be played out. They are packaged goods sold for a few dollars yielding an experience of moments.

To try and elicit any meaning that drinkers may attach to their purchases Merkley and Partners conducted what they call Conflict Analysis research. This research starts from the assumption that beliefs can run deep and may not be easily surfaced by normal focus group research that generally asks such banal questions as "How do you feel about this brand?" In order to force individuals to articulate what they feel deep down, they're put into a position where they are under attack. They are impelled to defend what they believe. In this situation they can become amazingly articulate, even about sugar water.

In Conflict Analysis, two groups are run simultaneously in adjacent rooms. Each group in this case represented drinkers recruited on the basis of frequency of consumption. The brands that they said they preferred the most were Snapple, SoBe, and Arizona Rx.

Each group eventually learned that there was another next door that drank a different beverage from their own. The group meetings were long: three hours (sometimes longer at the respondents' request). They were told that after the first hour-and-a-half, they would have to write a manifesto for their group, and present that declaration in a Death Match (named after the popular MTV animated show where celebrities fight to the finish) to the group next door. They would have to defend their manifestos against attack from members of a competitive brand community.

During the first half of the session they were given various exercises to help them articulate any potential commonalities of the group beyond their soft drink purchase habits and see whether there was any alignment between the group values and those of the brand. The groups were very lightly moderated (there was no discussion guide). The moderator was there simply to explain the exercises and goad them into beating the group next door.

The idea was to find out if the respondents could discover the hidden meaning behind their solidarity and beyond their purchase habits. Could the brand hold any higher meaning for them other than it "tastes great"? How would the group dynamics play out in ninety minutes? Would the group form into a cohesive community, would they be able to articulate what they believed, or would

everyone splinter off into their individual interests or solitary bore-
dom? Would the respondents not play the game, would they think
it a silly exercise?

In the end the manifestos clearly articulated a well-differentiated
worldview for the brands. For example, the SoBe drinkers described
a value system of tolerance and open-mindedness. For them the
brand (and themselves) could juggle an apparent paradox of high
energy with Zenlike meditation. One young DJ from Seattle said
SoBe's belief system was somewhere between "Yoko Ono and snowboarding." SoBeings (their self-description) felt no pressure to
conform to one idea of themselves or another: they could safely
"meditate and play extreme sports." Their manifesto read:

> Life is too short to be narrow-minded.
> Not limit ourselves to any one reality.
> Adventure, spontaneity and fun.
> Embrace all cultures and all living things and all people.
> Energize the body, uplift the spirit and enlighten the
> mind.

Snapple drinkers thought SoBe advocates had been hood-
winked, that they were the unconscious and foolish victims of marketing. Do they really think the drink makes them freer? In a
complex relationship between the brand's image of authenticity
and their own, Snapple drinkers knew they were being sold to by
marketers and because they knew, that made it all right.

> We the drinkers of Snapple Elements declare ourselves
> to be diverse individuals, bamboozled by the man and
> aware of it.

Arizona drinkers in all of the groups saw themselves as prag-
matic and self-aware (everyone else thought they were a little pe-

dantic), especially when it came to what they put in their bodies. They took the health claims on the bottles branded Rx seriously, examining and choosing them for their desired effect. Their manifesto read:

> We're healthy and active . . . educated especially on health issues . . . we think about our actions before we do them. We know what we need and don't need . . . but we're responsible for what we put in our bodies.

The definition of the brands and the drinkers' group identity were well developed. Respondents gave clear articulations of their brand's meaning system, especially when their manifestos came under attack. Some manifestos were even written in the form of the Declaration of Independence.

This technique flushes out any meaning that may be lurking unconsciously within buyers of the brand. To be sure, the Snapple drinkers' alignment with the idea of authenticity is likely to have been informed by the advertising that communicated the product's realness. But the other two brands offered little marketing communication from which they could have taken a lead. The Conflict Analysis methodology works especially well in parity categories. The meaning-based differences may not be readily apparent and are unlikely to be mined by conventional focus group research. It's a lab-based technique to observe community creation and belief articulation in real time (respondents often make arrangements to meet each other after the group, although previous to the session they were complete strangers) and from which you could get a head start in creating your brand's or cult's belief system.

Cults and cult brands must have meaning systems. For brands, they can be the source of differentiation, and in turn an opportunity to charge a premium without relying on the vicissitudes of product superiority. You can pluck meaning systems from the culture around you and adapt them for your own organization. You can surf on and steal existing beliefs held by various subcultures and appropriate those groups. Or you can give voice to a buried belief system within existing members of your community. Meaning systems should provide interpretation, give purpose, and create a sense of control or certainty.

8

SYMBOLISM

B rands are symbols. We live in a world dominated by commercial icons, total design initiatives, and completely integrated marketing efforts, where products are consumed less for what they *are* (materially) and more for what they *represent* (spiritually, or at least socially). We operate in a symbolic economy. It's one where crass products and their meaningless material benefits can be transformed into living vessels of meaning.

What are symbols and why are they so important? Symbols literally make meaning possible; they allow a given worldview to come alive in any and *in every* community. Symbols are the very stuff of culture, whether they are written, verbal, aural, or pictorial. They are the diverse media by which humans actively and outwardly communicate, celebrate, and protect their beliefs and values. Communities make meaning through public, symbolic expression: They sing it. Dance it. Burn it. Eat it. Wear it. Tattoo it on their face, and shave on their heads. "The unity of a group, like all its cultural values, must find symbolic expression," writes sociologist R. M. MacIver, "the symbol is at once a . . . means of communication and a common ground of understanding. All communication whether through language or other means, makes use of symbols. Society could scarcely exist without them."[1]

Symbols aren't just simple one-off icons—the cross, the star, the big-bellied Buddha. They're more like a network of signs that tie together an entire set of meaning. Clothes can be symbolic, so can music, food, and behaviors. Historically, these symbolic systems have been generated by cults and religions. From the first human societies onward, cults actively and consciously created distinct cultures through the orchestrated and integrated use of symbolic codes.

Beliefs are well and good in theory—scriptural truths, mission statements, enduring values and beliefs. In the end, however, ideas fade and only action remains. We are what we do, not what we think. For example, for Hare Krishnas, abstaining from alcohol and drugs, gambling, illicit sexual behaviors, and the eating of meat, fish, or eggs aren't just pie-in-the-sky *moral* dictates from a five-thousand-year-old God. They're symbolic behaviors, lived day in and day out by over tens of thousands of Krishna devotees worldwide. Chanting, singing, dressing, bathing, shaving, everything a Krishna does and says, everything he touches, wears, eats, or looks at is strictly designed to remind and inspire the devotee's loyalty to Krishna-consciousness. Those who fully buy into the Krishna way become totally saturated with symbols of the choice they've made.

Up until the 1960s, cults like the Hare Krishnas and established religions like Catholicism provided the lion's share of symbols and cultures for communities around the world. The fact that brands, and specifically cult-brands supply symbolic meaning to a vast majority of today's global citizens is a relatively late, although extremely important, historical development. Over the last hundred or so years, brands more or less functioned as they did from their inception. Marks of authenticity for services and goods. Trademarks for corporate property. Certainly not as symbolic systems for culture. What happened? It's important to answer that question if we want to truly exploit the opportunity it presents to us as marketers, communication companies, and commercial designers of all sorts.

The American Marketing Association defines the word "brand" as "a name, term, symbol, or design or a combination of these, which is intended to identify goods or services of one seller or group of sellers and to differentiate them from those of competitors."[2]

The AMA's definition of a brand is roughly one hundred or so years too old. Its origins reach back to beer and life in British pubs. Up until the middle of the nineteenth century, beer drinkers in England had been accustomed to getting their ale from their own local brewery. The Industrial Revolution changed all that: technology caused products to proliferate, and the railroad increased the range of distribution for those products. Meaning more products everywhere. These products had no local connection to consumers. There was no innkeeper to complain to if the beer was soapy, and no way of ensuring in the traditional manner (watching the man you trust brew your beer) that this was the same delicious brew that you'd enjoyed for years.

Breweries, isolated from their drinkers, began to mark their products with a signature of "origin" and "authenticity" in an attempt to make their pint special, local, and knowable.[3] In 1875, the United Kingdom passed the first TradeMark Bill, a piece of legislation designed to protect "genuine" symbols of authenticity. The Bass Red Triangle registered itself that same year, becoming, for all intents and purposes, the first symbol to legally signify a product's legitimacy in an increasingly impersonal world. The first brand.

A brand still functions as a symbol of authenticity and legitimacy just as it did in height of the Industrial Revolution. However, things have revolutionized even more since the time steam engines hauled beer and a consumer could only choose from four soaps, two or three car brands, and several different beers. Following the Second World War, and particularly around the 1960s, historical patterns of consumption changed irrevocably. For the first time in American economic history, supply outstripped demand.

Oscar winning producer and one time copywriter, Lord David Putnam, put it like this: "When I started my career in 1958, the components of advertising were really very simple, very unsophisticated— a product, a logo, a price, a stock list, and a claim. Things had changed by the mid-sixties. I guess it was around then that ads began to set out to convince human beings that their 'lifestyle' required certain products which they'd possibly never heard of, let alone thought about, and that, for the most part, they almost certainly didn't need. This was the beginning of what I'd now term 'consumer advertising,' and it involved a completely different approach."[4]

One of the most famous symbols in the commercial world that referenced a whole lifestyle was started with a campaign launched in 1959 by a now famous Madison Avenue shop called Doyle Dane Bernbach (DDB). The business objective seems unbelievable in retrospect. Turn a technically outdated, air-cooled, rear-engined Nazi car into a viable competitor in a market where consumers measured satisfaction by the size of a tail fin and the yardage of chrome.

DDB's Volkswagen Beetle campaign changed the game. Bill Bernbach eschewed obvious product-inspired marketing and instead turned to the power of social psychology and humor. Bernbach transformed what appeared to be a serious material disadvantage (the car's seemingly puny stature and lack of gizmos) into a symbol of an alternative American lifestyle. He told the disaffected and the disenchanted that it was okay to "Think Small." "By stressing humor, irony, truth, and simplicity, the ad agency targeted an informal coalition of environmentalists, ecologists, intellectuals, radicals, rebels, and free thinkers that DeSoto, Hudson, Packard, and Edsel had never imagined existed."[5]

Four decades later, in a research facility in the advertising capital of the world I'm listening to a professor, a house painter, a social worker, and third grade teacher named Simone play back Bernbach's marketing strategy almost exactly. It was as if it was some kind of grassroots movement they had invented themselves. The irony here is startling and important. It speaks to the degree that cult brand symbols can be perfectly embedded into the "self" of a community. "It was *ours*. When we saw someone else driving a VW, we knew what they stood for. And when you saw one of the tanks they called Cadillacs, you knew who was probably driving that car, and what they stood for."

From the Bernbach era onward, commercial messaging pressure has grown at an ungodly rate, creating a consumer culture arguably more Catholic than the symbolical world of organized religion (a cultural force uncontested for millennia). As the economy shifts from supply-side to demand-side, so too does the social importance of the brand. A mere half a century ago, it was the producer that the brand legitimized—the origin and authenticity of the product. Today a brand legitimizes the consumer—the *individual's and community's* origin and authenticity. A brand is no longer a flat sign for corporate identification, a two-dimensional logo plastered on the outside of a bottle. Brands are distinctive markers of human identity. They have become so important as cultural representations that people even brand them on their own body much as our predecessors tattooed symbols of social spiritual status. Why? Lee Clow, Chairman of TBWA Worldwide and creative developer of Apple's "Think Different" campaign explains:

"Brands aren't just a way of remembering what you want to buy any more. They've become part of the fabric of our society. Brands are part of our system of ordering things—they even create context about who we are and how we live. . . . They articulate who you are and what your values are."[6]

Of course the original Beetle is a primitive vehicle of meaning when compared to the integrated symbolic systems companies are now devising for their brands. The market is more complicated and crowded than it was a half-decade ago, and its customers are more symbol-literate. Companies must offer more than a stand-alone product that conveys meaning like some solitary crucifix. Cult-brand marketers know that they must colonize every single moment of everyday life. Their mission is to brand a living *experience,* to create a unified meaning system that transforms every possible touch-point between the company and the customer into symbol that refers back to a single idea or belief. Like a Hare Krishna temple.

On a crisp blue day in the early summer months of 2003, I walked past the Apple store on Prince Street in New York and saw a crowd of people spilling onto the street. It must be a fantastic sale, I thought, and eased my way in. In the store hundreds of faces were uplifted in rapture. Not at the prospect of a good deal, (despite being New Yorkers) they were actually looking at a gigantic screen. On it Steve Jobs was being beamed live delivering a sermon about his newest products, especially the G5, and how it fitted into the Macintosh family. Some people were transcribing his words in their BlackBerrys and e-mailing their friends as he spoke. Others just watched and listened, engrossed. You may think these were sad little geeks. They weren't. In the congregation was a mixture of people from the Tri-State area, ranging from older New York women in black with expensive haircuts to children, scrubbed executives, and the odd hippie.

The Prince Street venue is a temple of symbolic integration not unlike the amazing storefront of the Krishna Ashram on the Bowery not far away. Every sign and signal, every product and employee in the "store" is integrated into the larger system of Apple symbolism.

As you enter, you are faced with a stunning but simple glass staircase. On the first floor there are side chapels dedicated to the worship of digital photography, MP3s, and sleek laptops. Upstairs is the confessional—the Apple bar—where past mistakes are corrected and absolved on software misuse and hardware abuse. Worshippers' doubts are heard and some truths and answers are given here too. Along the galleries are the ecclesiastical libraries of software, and the sacred texts—the manuals and user guides. And everywhere, ministering quietly and reverentially, are the black clad acolytes, always on hand to explain the doctrine of loading software or give instruction on downloading music. At the top of the stairs you enter an inner sanctum. Congregants quietly gather there on slick pews facing a pulpit to the left of a giant flat screen exploding with color and life. The pastor of the day (the sermons are advertised on handouts given to you as you leave the store) will preach on the doctrine of OS X, the uses of Adobe Photoshop, the salvation of FinalCut.

Off to the right of the entrance is the altar, the last stop for a member's hour of supplication. A long smooth plinth of light colored wood, cash registers accept offerings from the dedicated, mediated by the smiling deacons.

The importance of Prince Street is that it is a representation, an *experiential* nexus of the corporation's, and community's beliefs—not just a playground or entertainment complex. It's a Mecca for customers to bathe in a completely integrated symbolic world. It's just one part of Apple's highly integrated symbolic system for a distinct community. What makes the iPod so successful, for instance, isn't just the way it perfectly fits into OS X, or into iTunes. It's how the sleek instrument intuitively plugs into a community's distinct meaning system and corollary symbolic code (the intuitive simplicity, the love of beauty, and the belief in creative power). The iPod, the iMac, iBook, all work together seamlessly with the advertising, the events, the Web site, and the temple on Prince Street. That is how a cult-brand works.

For the community, the symbolic system is a binding system. It beacons a group identity through a shared difference. Patrick put it this way: When you see a Mac, he said, "right away you get the image of the whole eccentric, outside-of-the-norm thing . . . things a lot of Mac users pride themselves on. And I think the fact the Mac looks so different, it's kind of attention grabbing, it's like 'look at this. This is not a PC. This is not a beige box, this is something special, this is something different from the norm.' "

People can be part of the symbolic structure of the brand too. Like Christ, Mohammed, or Buddha, individuals can be elevated to representational status in the brand world as much as the religious. In a society driven by brand symbols it would indeed be strange for there to be no commercial messiahs fulfilling the role of meaning-vessels. I asked a group of sane, stable, very self-aware Apple users what Steve Jobs represents. Clay claimed that "it all kind of emanates from one person . . . the whole kind of mythology and lifestyle."

How important a symbol is Jobs? Clearly in Clay's mind, a significant one, but also in his heart too. I asked what would happen if Jobs got knocked over by a bus. "I'd be massively . . . not hurt, but I'd be like worried . . . I don't know the exact emotion I'd feel . . . whatever it was, it would be intense. On some level it would be like losing someone you would personally know. I would be definitely upset."

Greg nodded and said: "I think I'd feel the same way. I mean it's strange how you'd be emotionally affected. He's like the human symbol of the company. When you think of Apple as a person, you think of Steve Jobs. Whether you like him or not, he's a big part of its identity."

There are, of course, distinct dangers to including real people in the symbolic system. For example, they might get run over by a bus. Living symbols have the advantage of being objects with which a membership can readily identify simply by virtue of being human, albeit elevated to demigod status. But like the fallible gods of the Ancient world, human symbols can trip, and bring your brand-meaning down with them (as I write Martha Stewart's dilemma is also creating one for her brand).

There are also dangers in creating a symbolic system that is, well, symbolic of nothing. Aesthetics are not enough. Icons are only icons because they communicate a world of meaning to the community that honors them. In an artful celebration of two the brands' similar aesthetics, VW has recently aired a beautifully constructed commercial advertising a free iPod with a Beetle, ending with the line "Pods Unite." I like the commercial. The camera almost caresses the smooth rounded lines of the products to, as always for both brands, a cool piece of music.

But this would have been so much more if both brands had equal status as cult brands. I would argue that VW's reincarnation in the new Beetle is not a cult-brand. While the body of the car is as distinctive as it ever was, material differences (no matter how extreme) do not a cult brand make. The New Bug does not *mean* anything. Its strange, space like features don't *represent* any group's belief, unlike its meaning-rich predecessor. Unless material differences explicitly symbolize a difference in values and beliefs, then all you've got is an interesting shaped product. Instead of a commercial trumpeting the unification of two community's parallel belief systems in a powerful assault against the mainstream, "Pods Unite" is a sort of a "yeah we look alike, cool isn't it?" announcement.

Get over your products. Get an integrated symbolic system. Get over the plastic, the wires, the fillers, and the ingredients. (Products are price of entry.) Think about the symbol system you're making possible instead—that is where you'll find true and lasting differentiation. What kind of environment are you providing that will allow your customers a place to commune with their fellow believers and the distinct symbols of their belief? What Temple to what god are you creating?

9 COMMITMENT IS A TWO-WAY STREET

Cults define the idea of commitment in the popular mind. Cult members are perceived to be devoted beyond any social norm. Their extremism triggers wonder in many, repellence in others, and envy in those who want to elicit similar devotion to their own organizations.

Contrary to most popular assumptions, cult members' commitment may be fierce, but it is not blind. At the end of the day, their attachment is the function of an exchange. For all of the benefits of belonging that we've covered in this book—a community, the ability to make meaning, self-actualization—the member has paid a price. The opportunity cost of belonging to a cult is high. Time, emotion, money, careers, respect, and often family and relationships have been surrendered to the organization. If that committment is not matched by an equivalent reward, including the feeling that the leadership is as committed and has paid an equal price, then the results can be disastrous for the cult.

This concept of "the trade of commitment" is equally true in the world of business. For cultlike devotion to a brand, there must be a corresponding investment from the company. Sean, an impecunious student felt committed enough to his brand to "feel almost personally responsible for the well being of the Mother Company. I find with Apple . . . I'm much more prone to buy directly from Apple rather than through a reseller. Just because you want . . . you want Apple to get everything . . . it's like, take my money."

He is a marketer's dream.

But this immoderate devotion can be spoiled. Anger a committed devotee and you have a brand terrorist on your hands: Sean continued: "We talked about people being really interested in the well-being of Apple. I think there's an opposite direction to that . . . when Apple does something really stupid or really obnoxious or they make some big mistake. I've seen people get personally offended by it, like they feel betrayed somehow or insulted that Apple has done this."

The rewards of creating cultlike devotion are high. But so are the potential dangers. There must be mutual investment present in the high stakes of a cult relationship.

We will now look at three dramatic examples of betrayal, one within a classic cult and the other two within famous mass cult brands. In the first two examples the betrayal was a surprisingly frequent and nearly always catastrophic mistake made by the leadership. They lied to their followers. In these examples the community's faith in the truth of the cult's meaning system was abused by the actions of the leadership. They didn't walk the talk. In the third, the company—Apple—managed to recommit itself to its customers and thus save its brand. During the dark days prior to the resurrection of Steve Jobs, the loyalty of the Apple community was gradually worn down by years of neglect and abuse. We'll look at this less startling, but equally damaging dereliction of duty to the cult membership. And we'll also examine what was done to remedy the problem.

In the process of examining these examples, we'll also note how people become committed (beyond the core attractions already covered—belonging, meaning, etc.). We'll look at how important it is to match the cost of staying and to make the cost of leaving high.

An Abuse of Commitment

"I remember my mom messed up, like crying and trying to explain it to me . . . like it was a really big thing . . . the pain of leaving like that. It was horrible." Bella was fifteen years old when she was wrenched from the life she had known since the age of three. She, her mother, and stepfather were leaving the Fellowship of Friends, a cult that had as many as three thousand members worldwide, whose population lives in houses in groups of twelve or fifteen in the best neighborhoods (you might be living on the same street as one right now). Bella is now an actress and singer living in New York. She has a pixieish beauty, with a transfixing stare. Her life up to that day had been totally dominated by the Fourth Way, a philosophy taught and applied by the charismatic, and now disgraced leader, Robert Earl Burton.

The output of the largest commune of the cult, a place called Apollo, is a famed wine that is served in the best restaurants in the world (Ronald Reagan is known to be partial to it). The product is symbolic of the ethos of the cult. Like The Work, the Fellowship follows the teachings of Gurdjieff and Ouspensky, who taught that individuals must jolt themselves out of the waking sleep of everyday existence to elevate themselves to a higher consciousness. The Fellowship's interpretation of this often meant consuming the best of everything in order to rise above the everyday.

Bella described how, when her parents were running the cult's house in Forest Hills, New York (an upscale suburb), they would attend the opera and plays, and once a month go to a five-star restaurant. Burton preached that you must constantly disrupt normality into a state of "self-remembering," that you must always be conscious of the moment. Bella related a surreal and humorous attempt to stimulate her consciousness when, in a swanky restaurant, her mother Margot took off her shoe and put it on top of her head so that her daughter would "always remember this moment." She did. Bella explained the philosophy as follows. "There are four states of consciousness. The first is when you're asleep. The second is when you're 'waking sleep' [the state most nonmembers are in], the third is when you are really awake when you are living in the moment. The fourth is when you're in total higher consciousness, awake, awake."

But being stimulated to the third or fourth state was not always done in so charming a manner as the shoe story, or by consuming the best of everything. Burton, following in the footsteps of Gurdjieff, "liked to make things hard for people." He would tell members to dig a hole and then fill it in again, a process called "friction." The demands went further, ranging in edicts from forbidding people to say the word "I" to forbidding them to have children.

Margot, whom I also interviewed, had to make a similar sacrifice. She and her husband were relatively early recruits to The Fellowship. When they arrived at Renaissance (the former name for Apollo) in the hills of Northern California, it was nothing but a few huts. They slept in sleeping bags on the floor and built the place by hand. They rose up the hierarchy and were commissioned to start and run branch communes in major cities in the United States. That meant that every time Burton commanded, they had to resign whatever jobs they had outside the commune, uproot, and start over.

She bitterly regrets it now, but when they were about to run the Miami center, and Margot worried about uprooting her daughter, Burton told her "if you put your work and yourself first, your daughter will learn from that, and she will value that also for herself." He instructed Margot to send Bella away to her grandparents and she acquiesed.

According to Margot she and her husband "were never coerced to stay," even though they paid high financial as well as emotional prices. All members had to tithe 10 percent of their wealth to the cult and some people had to do two jobs to meet some of the additional financial demands that Burton made. Why did they do it? When the times were good, they had "emotional bonds that were deep and strong" with "wonderful people." They could go virtually anywhere in the world and stay at one of the cult's houses where "we welcomed one another . . . we just had the comfort that the other people understood that we were all working on the same thing": the Fourth Way, a path to enlightenment and self-fulfillment.

But they eventually realized that their own commitment to the cult's way of life and philosophy was not matched by their leader's. Burton had got a good deal out of the cult. In the spirit of being stimulated by the best things of life, he drank the best wines, ate the best food, flew on Concorde to visit his schools in Europe, and surrounded himself, and the rest of the commune, with sculptures and paintings worth millions. While he was dressed in the best clothes, many followers could not afford dental work.

The leeway that the cult members had been giving Burton was demolished by a revelation triggered by a sex scandal. As Bella put it "it turned out that he was taking advantage of a lot of people. He was accused of socking away a lot of the contributions made by his followers." He had issued an order that "no-one was to be gay, homosexuality was bad and that gay students had to stop immediately." But at the same time "he used his power" to "take advantage of men . . . but straight men . . . it messed a lot of people up." Some of these people left the cult and sued him, attracting much negative publicity.

Why did Margot and her family not leave earlier? She was aware of the sacrifices she was making; yet it took evidence of betrayal to weaken her devotion and leave. "I guess it was like, you know, the story of the frog in warm water," she said. If you put a frog into a pot of boiling water it will leap out immediately. However, if you put a frog into a pot of cold water and gradually heat it up, it will stay there until it dies unaware of the slowly changing circumstances.

The cost of leaving for a cult member is normally very high. Margot's family had given up much in terms of finance, emotions, and time. To walk away from such an investment is hard. "We've sacrificed all that, and with nothing to show for it."[1]

They would also be leaving members of a community that had essentially become their family. And the separation would be absolute. Burton had issued an edict that those who remained would have no contact with those who left. Margot and her family knew that they would be estranged in just the same way as they had cut off others who had chosen to leave. As Bella remembers, "We would be walking around Manhattan and she [her mother] would see somebody she knew and had left and she wouldn't be able to talk to them. She would just look through them. It was against the rules. It was a really big thing."

Some religions threaten backsliders with hell or exile. So do some commercial organizations with strong belonging cultures. Procter and Gamble threatened that I would never be able to come back if I resigned. And I would want to come back, because "out there" was mediocrity, "in here" was the best you can get. The threat of being ostracized, of settling for second best, even damnation if you leave is common technique of member retention.

In strong commitment organizations there is a cost to leaving as much as there is a cost to staying. An organization needs to ensure that the reward for staying is perceived to be equivalent to the cost.

The Cost of Commitment Is Initially Low

How do people become committed in the first place? They don't suddenly wake up one day and say "I'm going to give up my house, my family and my career for this organization that I heard about just yesterday." Do they?

It's all about the frog in warm water. Bella's family's entry process was gradual and demanded small sacrifices. It cost only thirty dollars per couple when they joined, but grew in increments until "we spent enormous amounts of money." Time and emotional commitment were also small to begin with. In the early stages, interested individuals attended classes on Ouspenky's and Gurdjieff's teachings at schools. They "didn't feel as if they had to make a total commitment. If you like the first classes you could become more committed if you wanted to." Of course, as they became gradually more involved they formed friendships with other members. The "Power of the Person" took over and by the time a significant commitment was made, it was to new friends and "family," not just an organization.

The Cost of Lying

Let's go back to The Body Shop. Throughout the 1980s and early 1990s, business schools and periodicals across the nation touted the wild success of The Body Shop, praising Anita Roddick's unorthodox beliefs about business and ethics, her commitment to principles that transcend the ordinary profit-motives of large corporations. Roughly ten years later—ten years after Anita Roddick became an overnight millionaire, ten years after The Body Shop climbed to the red-hot top of the London Stock Exchange—it all came crumbling down. In 1994, a relatively unknown freelance writer named John Entine wrote an article for a niche magazine called *Business Ethics*[2] (incidentally one of Roddick's favorites, given its focus on corporate social responsibility). Point by point, the article methodically laid out a long and winding trail of lies, inconsistencies, and broken commitments, a Body Shop based on profits, not principles.

Entine blew up the whole founding mythology of the Shop—
wild hippie Anita starting up on a shoestring with the odd ingredients she picked up on exotic, third world travel. In truth, according
to Entine, Roddick never scoured the world for natural scents and
emollients—she appropriated the idea wholesale from a family friend
who ran a dingy boutique she visited in San Francisco circa 1970. It
was called The Body Shop (she bought the rights to the name from
her friend later), and it sold hand-labeled bottles filled with cosmetics and natural lotions from around the world. "Comparisons
of the brochures of the American original and Roddick's copy-
cat store are telling," wrote Entine. "Four O'clock Astringent Lotion morphed into Five O'clock Astringent Lotion. Korean Washing
Grains, uniquely developed by the women who sewed kimonos for
the Americans, became Japanese Washing Grains ... Roddick
copied product descriptions word-for-word, including grammati-
cal errors."

And that's just the beginning. Roddick built an entire empire on
this original lie, a radical commitment to grassroots beauty and
business that, with each new initiative, with each new product,
amassed incredible loyalty for her brand, but, according to her crit-
ics, amounted to little more than a marketing ploy. Roddick's central claim was about her products. ("We can't and shouldn't be
grouped together with the myriad of other companies crying 'natural!' " Roddick preached, "Because as you probably know, we're not
like other companies.") Totally natural and acquired responsibly
from indigenous sources: these powerful, differentiating assertions,
according to Entine and now many former Body Shop customers,
were total fabrications.

From opening day in 1976, The Body Shop's unique bottles were
filled with nonrenewable petrochemical-based ingredients like
mineral oil, petrolatum, carbomers, and isopropyl mysristate. "Those
ingredients are still in today's products. . . . As the company evolved
from a hippie storefront in Brighton into a growing English con-

cern and finally into an international cosmetic company . . . synthetic ingredients were introduced as preservatives to provide long-term stability of its products. Roddick filled her products with bright dyes and artificial fragrances. Over time, the brightly colored, heavily fragranced lotion became as much a part of the company's trademark as its natural reputation," Entine wrote.

And just where did these chemicals come from? In the Reagan-era 1980s when other corporations were raping the globe for resources, Roddick differentiated her company by banging the pulpit for fair trade, good global citizenry, and corporate social responsibility. "Consumers are increasingly aware that their purchases are moral choice," Roddick explains in her Manifesto-Autobiography *Business as Unusual*, "The Body Shop believes that trading should be an ethical act. Fair trade is absolutely central to us. It means we have to avoid the direct exploitation of humans and animals and avoid any negative impact on their habitats. And knowing that environments, and the people in them, are not exploited means we can give consumers the information to choose more responsibly."

In a text he developed to defend himself against Body Shop's legal vengeance, Entine spells out about a half-a-dozen bogus fair trade initiatives, rife with exploitation and hypocrisy.[3] Footsie-rollers made in an Indian orphanage turned sweatshop. Rainforest bath beads supplied "by some of the most rapacious, anti-environmental firms in Latin America including the Mutran family which has been linked to killing union leaders in the southern Amazon and employing slave labor." The violations run like a laundry list. "The lie is what upsets me," the Director of Amanakaa Amazon Relief Agency comments on The Body Shop's fair trade policies: "They're not helping the Kayapo Indians. It's all a show. First world wages? They pay first world wages all right—the same dirt-cheap wages other first world companies pay. They're worse than United Fruit. Anita Roddick is lying about how she helps the rainforest, but who would believe some Brazilian activists?"

"Improper bacteria sampling procedures," "Contaminated Banana Shampoo," "Contaminated Foot Scrub," "Elderflower Eye Gel problems," "Bacteria on filling machines," "Rancid products," "Formaldehyde in cosmetics": Entine's work on The Body Shop (he's written several articles to date) reads like a cult deprogrammer. Cult deprogrammers or intervention specialists, as they're known, follow an exacting method by which each and every lie and broken commitment is spelled out in plain English, until the member is forced to question everything the cult says and does.

Deprogrammers take cult members through all the spiritual texts, commandments, and values of the cult and show the inconsistencies between what the leaders preach and what they actually practice. One-by-one the truths and principles of the cult are encountered, examined, and systematically deconstructed.[4] And that's exactly what Entine did. "Consumers buy The Body Shop's pricey shampoos and lotions," wrote Entine, "because they believe . . . the company practices what it preaches."

In a world when criticism can be hurled around the Internet, anyone can discover and publicize the inconsistencies and untruths of any establishment. The World Wide Web is littered with hundreds of ex-cult sites, where spurned initiates can share stories about how they were hurt, lied to, and abused. In the consumer world, grass-roots consumer-advocacy sites like PlanetFeedback function in a similar way (customers can log onto an online community and warn the world about companies that have lagged on their commitment). Brand-loyalists become brand-terrorists with a single punch of the return key. In today's world, the faintest smell of hypocrisy from a commitment-based organization will surely become a PR debacle overnight. It's the anti-advocacy effect, writ short, "Hell hath no fury like a cult-member spurned."

The Price of Neglect

Patrick had a "strange, irrational need for Apple to succeed. I want them to do better and I want them to gain more market share." He didn't always feel this way. I talked to him and some other Mac users who had been through the "dark days," and (lucky for Apple) had come out the other side.

They admitted that the Apple brand had a near miss during the dark days and that it had forced them to seriously review their commitment. As Lou puts it, "back in '96 when things were hitting rock bottom and I remember thinking 'what's with these people, what's happening here?' " They were "pretty archaic for a while . . . my Apple wasn't much compared to the new PCs that were coming out that my friends had."

This is a story of betrayal through neglect. And it's also one of recovery by a recommitment of the leadership to the people. It is possible to "re-cult" a brand that is dying, but it requires absolute focus and uncompromised energy to reestablish the lost trust.

Your company or brand may not have endured the kind of crisis that The Body Shop or Fellowship of Friends experienced. Not all commitment problems come in such obvious or blatant forms. More commonly (which is to say, very commonly), they are the result of everyday organizational inertia—minor concessions, group think, and general lassitude. Every time a limp idea is chosen for political expediency, every time a mediocre message is approved out of fear, every time vision and care is subsumed by mechanism and compromise, there you'll find an institution slowly rotting at the core and quickly alienating its core constituents.

Steve Jobs's baby slowly rotted in this way throughout his long exile. It was not necessarily because the company lacked a pop-icon

CEO like Jobs but because the company lost its original commitment and vision and became distracted by quarterly results and foolhardy product development.

Everyone fondly remembers 1984 and the Superbowl commercial that launched a global icon. Yet nearly a decade later, Apple was essentially unrecognizable as the company that so boldly trumpeted its vision of a better world. A movement that generated the intense loyalty of groupies around the country was but a shadow of its former self. The only thing that remained was the premium price—not the ingenious and easy-to-use software, not the beauty and uncommon aesthetics of its hardware. The Apple of the 1980s was clunky and run by corporate men as beige as the dull machines it manufactured during these years.

Some observers believe that the introduction of the iMac series of computers saved Jobs and his company. More important, the CEO made a conscious decision to recommit. He threw himself back into the community, reciprocating his constituents' energy with his own. He was "investing in me . . . I think he understands Mac users [unlike the inter-regnum management] that's why the company has done so much better under him" as Greg claimed. They saw their devotion mirrored by their leader.

Not only did Jobs recommit to the community with product; he did it by acutely understanding that the cult membership was buying into an idea. Previous to his return, the company had been in a tailspin without vision and the product that lived that vision. Jobs quickly pulled the brand out of this catastrophic dive by actually reinvesting in the ideology prior to the launch of the iMac. In a typically radical move, soon after his return to the company he cut the R&D staff by about 80 percent and shuttled the money to Chiat/Day, the communications company that crafted the famous 1984 commercial. At MacWorld, where he launched the Think Different campaign and the iMac, he publicly reset the course of the brand. The following is an excerpt from his speech to software developers and dealers:

"Marketing is about values. We have to be very clear on what we want our customers to know about us. They want to know who is Apple and what do we stand for. What we're about is not making boxes for people to get their jobs done, although we do that very well. Apple is about more than that. What Apple is about, its core value is that we believe that people with passion can change the world for the better. That's what we believe." The commercial, featuring clips of Picasso, Branson, Einstein, and others begins: "Here's to the crazy ones . . ."

In short, the company was finally fulfilling its part of the bargain by providing not just reinvigorated products, but by reestablishing a vision. Its products have rekindled Apple's reputation for shaking up the market (look how fast the beige box-makers copied the brightly colored iMac, the bestselling computer that year) and providing justification for the memberships' belief that they are different (and better than the rest of the world). And it even provides sustenance when they are persecuted for their deviance. According to Patrick he gets "hassled" because "you're using something different from them," (PC users) and interestingly, he believes, they're jealous: "I think it's because they secretly know that they're wrong, they made the wrong decision [choosing a PC]. They know we're better. I mean, who ever says, 'Oh wow, you're using a Dell. No one ever says that.' " When Mac users get together they have plenty to share, including the mythology of their passionate crazy leader, who loves and is committed to them.

And the cherry on the top for Patrick was that Jobs has helped him to become a missionary once again. For brand advocates, their reputation is on the line when they make a recommendation. There must be the stuff there that warrants a conversion. In the case of Apple, the conversion and therefore the credibility of converter are significant. According to Patrick: "We are all somewhat different because we use a Mac, and I think that when you convert someone you feel like you maybe have changed them for life . . . it's really a massive deal . . . they need to be saved." Patrick needed to feel that his brand, and the commitment of leadership behind it, was up to midwifing the conversion.

Commitment Is a Lifetime Contract

As with any loving and real relationship, a company must continually commit to its customers, renew its beliefs with real product and service experiences every quarter. Apathy is the enemy in a cult relationship. Every action, every offering, every communication must be scrutinized for its commitment to the membership.

Check everything you do by the standard of fair trade: are you making a similar sacrifice (in terms of money, time, energy) as the cult member? Will whatever you are proposing jeopardize the commitment of the devoted (but not blind) membership? Playing the cult game is one of high stakes. You will get very high rewards, but they come at the cost of your commitment—your time, money, energy, ideas, and veracity. The highest cost of all (the cult's destruction) will be incurred if you scrimp on your side of the trade.

10

GO FORTH AND MULTIPLY

Do you want a large or small cult? This is not a facetious question. Most cult leaders start out expecting that they will capture a large following, yet most of what they proceed to do guarantees a small one. Cult leaders, whether of the religious or business variety, can be more successful if they do something foreign to their natures—be humble.

The Joy and Pain of Deviancy

Cults are inherently deviant.

Deviancy is good. It has the potential to change civilizations or markets if it succeeds in gaining a large and influential enough following. Without deviancy cultures and markets would grow tired and atrophy. And without difference, the cult will not attract those who are alienated from the establishment.

But too much deviancy can exclude a large potential audience. Moreover, cults can be destroyed by an establishment that is threatened by too much difference. They can be persecuted into oblivion. By managing deviancy well cult leaders could be as famous as Jesus

Christ or Mohammed. By managing it badly, they could be as infamous as David Koresh or Jim Jones.

Cults fail as seeds of cultural change if they fall on the stony ground of refusal by the common man. Cult brands also fail if they don't move relatively quickly beyond the early adopters to the majority of consumers, the ones who provide the real revenue and profit. It's all about managing deviancy and familiarity. To understand the ramifications of deviancy and growth, let's look at how new ideas are adopted.

The problem with new or different ideas is that people hate new and different ideas. The majority does anyway, and they are the only ones who count. Only early adopters relish the revolutionary, and they seldom make a long term, profitable business. They're always on to the next thing, and if they do stay for a limited time, they will demand innovation because by nature they enjoy anything novel. That is a costly consumer segment for any business to attempt to satisfy. It tends to be relatively small and it demands huge product development costs. What business really needs is to appeal to the majority, not just a small group of strange people who thrive on strangeness.

Your objective should be to focus acquisition investment on the conservative majority; those who are slow to adopt the new, but who, when they do, are slow to leave it. Thus, the challenge facing the marketer, the cult leader, the politician, or anyone intent on starting a new and different organization is to do the following. They must crack the conundrum of selling something *unfamiliar* to individuals who, at heart, want the *familiar.*

How do leaders avoid the handicap of the new? How can they build a strong attachment to their idea among a large and ordinary audience that is normally repelled by the strange?

Make the *Novel* Appear *Familiar*

This idea will be antithetical to most marketers and cult leaders. If you have something new, the accepted wisdom suggests, shout it to the world. Claim the crown of innovation. Be feted in business magazines as the new revolutionaries.

What makes better sense is to craft "buyable newness." The cults that have flourished have tempered newness. As a result they have attracted ordinary people to become mass-market organizations relatively quickly. They learned to modify their apparent difference in order to penetrate the mainstream culture. Successful revolutionaries are the ones who have figured out how to seduce the masses by making their proposition appear not so revolutionary.

Christianity, one of the most successful cults, achieved market leadership in a short span despite some radically new theology. Estimates suggest that by 300 A.D., roughly half the population of the Roman Empire was Christian, rendering it politically necessary for the Emperor Constantine to anoint it as the state religion. (This political decision has since been mythologized into a miraculous conversion story, in which Constantine witnessed a vision from God before a battle that he subsequently won, and that inspired him to convert.) The expansion of the cult to this point equates to a 40 percent growth rate per decade, fast in any terms, but especially for a culture-transforming idea. Mormonism is following almost exactly the same path. It is on track to be the next World Religion by 2080, and has also grown at 40 percent per decade over the past century, which will number it in the hundreds of millions by the middle of this one.

Both religions in their early period were the kind of cults that we would recognize today. They had ideologies that threatened the establishment, and dictated behavior that it found antisocial. And they were both chastised in their early period for being too deviant. Christ was crucified, and the Mormons fled to avoid persecution because they intimidated their neighbors with their strangeness.

So how did they recruit enough from the ranks of the ordinary to become major religions? They made themselves appear not so new.

If the idea you are proposing is radically new, defuse its strangeness by making it recognizable, to some degree. The counterintuitive strategy for business, religious, and political leaders is to eschew the vanity of claiming to have invented something completely new, and instead propose that you are simply improving on an already good idea.

We'll examine two ways of doing this. The first key strategy is to use the *membership* as a translator of the new. This route uses "The Power of the Person" that we discussed in chapter 3. Utilizing relationships to present a familiar face to an unfamiliar idea is an extremely potent recruitment strategy. It's what makes word of mouth the uncontested leader in effective media available to a marketer. The recruiter can be *literally* familiar (they are friends, family, colleagues or neighbors) or equally, they can be *figuratively* familiar—they are "like me." "If this person (who is like me) likes this product, I might too," is the essence of this approach. Or, "Mary Kay's story is like mine." "I connect with that person in that ad."

The second strategy is to craft the *ideology* and *practice* to appear as if it is built on the foundation of something already accepted. Thus, Christian teaching developed from Judaism, and Mormonism from Christianity. Swatch is like a conventional watch, but it's costume jewelry not Tiffany's; and Starbucks is like a continental café, but it's American, and with take-out. New, but yet somewhat familiar.

Familiarity Breeds . . . and Breeds

The most famous face of recruitment for the Mormon Church are the well-scrubbed and wholesome missionaries who work for two years anywhere in the world that they are sent. They are the *least effective* method of recruitment available to this *most successful* of contemporary cults, at least when they are used in the way most familiar to us: cold calling on the street or at people's doors. The church has recognized the power of social networks. They've utilized the productivity of existing relationships. In the words of Jayson, who was recalling his missionary assignment in Romania, "You know, somebody has joined the church, and they believe in it strongly . . . so they bring their friends to church, they send the missionaries to their parents or cousins or whatever. *The most effective way of finding new people is a personal referral.*"

In other words, the church recognizes the potential of using the rail tracks of social interaction already laid down by close-knit families and networks of friends to speed its new ideas. Kevin and Robert, two committed and charming young men currently on mission in New York, confirmed that the church places its "biggest emphasis for missionaries on *talking with friends of people who are already members of the church.* That's the biggest source of converts right there."

The church also knows the power of outreach in terms of forming social relationships *before* making the pitch of the new idea. Peggy Fugal, the agency founder in Salt Lake City, recalls that according to church lore:

> One in every one thousand people cold-contacted by a missionary joins the church.

> One in every five hundred people who knows a Mormon when contacted by a missionary joins the church.
>
> One in every two hundred fifty people who is referred to the missionary joins the church.
>
> One in every one hundred people who is befriended by a member joins the church.
>
> One in every fifty people who goes to church with a member joins the church.
>
> One in every twenty-five people who is taught by the missionaries in the home of a member joins the church.

She reports that the latter is the "goal and the focus in missionary work" and hence the Mormon adage: "every member is a missionary." Every member is a potent organ for the cult's procreation.

At its beginnings, the Mormon church accelerated to over 24,000 members in fourteen years from a base of preexisting social contacts. Joseph Smith, its founder, recruited its first members from his family and those of the surrounding population that was connected in some way to his immediate social circle.

In addition to using the power of social networks—*the potency of the person*—the Mormons also know the value of introducing an initially *defused doctrine*. The recruitment formula demands that their unique doctrine be presented *in the context of* common ideological ground. The two brave missionaries in downtown New York are very conscious of avoiding potentially alienating Mormon ideology at the first approach: "There's [sic] differences [of doctrine]. So we'll first try and focus on a lot of the similarities and get that established; a belief in Jesus Christ and God. And then we'll talk about things like the Book of Mormon and Joseph Smith."

There really are fundamental differences in ideology. They veer so radically that several of the world's major religions refuse to recognize the Mormon Church's baptisms as valid (including Catholics,

Presbyterians, and Methodists). Among the more innovative tenets are that God was once "as man is now" and that he developed a power and spirituality that all Mormons are enjoined to imitate and eventually reach. He has a divine wife. They believe that "Zion will be built upon the American continent."[1] Human beings were once spirit children who acquire physical form on earth for a period of testing prior to rejoining their family in one of several heavens.

This radical theology is not presented at first contact. Commonalities will be found when prospects are first approached (mutual friends, an interest in sports, and so on). If the prospect is interested in finding out more about the member's beliefs, six prescribed "presentations" are given that gradually introduce the Church's doctrine.

Officially, the name of the Church is The Church of Jesus Christ of Latter-day Saints. The name has been deliberately modified over time by church officials to emphasize its similarity to the established Christian religions. This tempering of the Church's essential difference can be useful in defusing a potentially negative response on first contact. As Robert related, "Sometimes I'll hear someone who will say you guys aren't Christian. But usually they'll change their mind after they look at the name of the church."

This normalization policy really geared up when the Winter Olympics were scheduled for Salt Lake City. Church leaders knew that the global media would be scrutinizing the religion as much as the games. They officially shortened the name to "The Church of Jesus Christ." Referring to it as the "Mormon Church" was no longer acceptable. Even now, on the organization's own materials, the words Jesus Christ are typographically emphasized at the expense of The Latter-day Saints. The church has mollified its oddness over time to outsiders. But its radical theology has not changed. Compared to its surrounding culture, it is still deviant. It has just crafted familiarity into its appearance as it penetrates further into mainstream society.

Let's look now at a mass cult brand. It was deviant—it represented a revolutionary new way to make and sell cars. But it gained enough of a following among the masses to create a revolution. Over a decade later the rest of the market is still copying its early, deviant practices. Saturn, like the Mormons, defused its radical difference by appearing familiar.

Saturn: A Familiar Kind of Car Company

"A different kind of company, a different kind of car." This mantra, hymned in all communications, was designed to promise a different kind of buying and ownership experience. Yet the appeal of the Saturn proposition to a large and unsatisfied buying population, was that at its heart, it was a difference that appeared profoundly familiar. It was a revolution undertaken by ordinary people. It was a radical idea executed by familiar faces. And behind it was an idea so familiar that it was impossible not to accept it.

One of the signature commercials shows a man (actually the General Manager, the real one) talking to camera: "It all started with a challenge for the old values . . . maintain the old values." He's a heartland kind of man, weathered and stoic, and embodies, you feel, all things that make America decent. To go back to the heart of things you have to start over, he argues, and to do that you have to go to a place where the employees will feel comfortable, because "you can't build cars without people." At this point there are lots of shots of the literal greenfield site for the plant—an icon of heartland America (although it happens to be Tennessee) with tractors, horses, fields all nestled around a small town called Springhill.

In another commercial (all of these have become part of the mythology of owner and employee alike, ten years after they were aired), the customer becomes an intimate within the community of employees at Springhill. Judith Reiswig, a third grade teacher, placed an order for a Saturn "after reading the *Time* magazine article." This homely woman, everyone's vision of an upstanding and sympathetic teacher, your auntie in chalk-dusted bifocals, explains that "I liked the whole idea of what Saturn was all about. It's one of the things I try and instill in my kids, so I hope its true. It reminded me a little bit of a mom and pop operation in the old days." She sends a picture of herself to the plant and finds it in the glove compartment signed by the team members who built her car.

The launch commercials spend very little time talking about the car. As the tagline suggests, it's the company that's important, and the company, the commercials insist, is the people. And what are these people like? They are like you and me. The commercials are an anthem to the unsophisticated wholesomeness of the average American, set in the bucolic context of the (increasingly lost) lodestone of unchanging values, rural America.

This campaign, in fact the whole Saturn idea, as Judith Reiswig explained, is an explicit appeal for trust in the face of newness. By returning to already accepted values of the culture—community, respect for individuals, pride in your work and ownership of its outcome, celebration of geographical communities, and family values—the dubious prospect of a new American car company was rendered acceptable.

The company and its communications juggled the paradox of familiarity and difference through all the points of contact with its customers. The most important of which is of course the dealerships. They are, in fact, not dealerships but "stores," an important distinction. Saturn wanted to connote a buying experience typical of other less pressured purchases, somewhere where the distressing ambiguity of a deal was removed. So they introduced the now famous no-haggle pricing policy.

By 1992, Saturn had sold nearly two hundred thousand cars in the United States in its second year, making it the tenth highest selling brand. It was being sold faster than it could be built. Seventy percent of Saturn's customers were new business for GM. Loyalty and word of mouth was high. A J.D. Power survey in 1992 measuring customer's predisposition to loyalty ranked Saturn fourth after three luxury brands: Lexus, Infiniti, and Cadillac.

In 1993 nearly half of the first time visitors to a Saturn showroom had been referred by a friend or family member. In other words, the power of the person had kicked in, giving the brand cult a relatively fast start by having new ideas presented by old faces. But it was the advertising that was the catalyst to this huge army of unpaid salespeople. The brand was being presented by familiar faces in the figurative sense; the people in the ads shared the values of the audience. They seemed familiar in very basic terms. They were figurative friends and family that articulated a different culture from what you expect when buying a car, but one that is profoundly familiar in terms of basic human values. In other words, the advertising was like mass word of mouth.

Does all of this mean that your cult should not be different? That it should be as close to its surrounding culture as possible? No. As I argued in chapter 2, difference is critical to a cult. The discontented need to find a community that has different values from the existing culture, one which disappoints them and in which they do not feel at home. This growth strategy of making the novel appear familiar is not a contradiction of the need to be different. It is about the *presentation* of difference at the first point of contact. The Mormons *appear* to be a regular Christian religion when you first meet them. It is only later that the true differences become apparent. Most of the recruits arrive at the cult's radical theology via the familiarity of a personal connection. By the time that the new belief system is revealed, the recruit has already formed relationships with people that they trust. It's a small leap from a trusted friend to their religion. If my friend thinks this is the right path, then there must be something to it, the typical logic goes. The prospect is likely to become a recruit (if they are not already committed to a religion) because the *novel* is made *familiar*.

11

TENSION: THE MANAGEMENT OF DEVIANCE

Tension can be one of the biggest challenges facing a cult leader. It is the single biggest intangible that needs to be understood and managed if you ever wish to see your cult flourish. Some religious sociologists have interpreted tension as a two-way street where cults not only reject society, but are, in turn, rejected by society.[1] Tension is, simply put, the dynamic continuum between these two acts of repulsion. At one extreme, a cult's deviance from the social norms can become so offensive that society cannot tolerate its existence. At the other, a cult might be so tame it becomes indistinguishable from its surroundings, rendering it indifferent and irrelevant.

You could employ all the tools taught in this book to create a cult brand, but if you neglect to properly manage its tension, your cult will die.

There are as many ways to manipulate tension as there are ways to be different or similar. You can be too different like Napster and be crushed by the recording establishment, or become overly familiar, like Snapple (which under Quaker Oats ownership lost its cult status and the stock price plummeted). The objective is to balance your brand's tension.

TOO MUCH TENSION

Perhaps the most tempting mistake is to push your cult too close to the edge. It is so easy to get caught up in your ideology and scream, "You're wrong, we hate you" to the establishment. But cults that are too different can be too threatening and the establishment won't hesitate to destroy them. It is a simple tactic that the dominant Christian Church, for example, has used countless times in the past to maintain its position. Pilgrims or Mormons, Cathars or Protestants were all, at some point, too tense and had to run for cover, suffer being burned, or simply cease to exist. When the church shouts "heresy" it is a sure indicator that there is a threatening level of tension.

In a more recent example, Falun Gong is in a highly tense state with the Chinese government. At one time supported by the authorities as a healthy practice, it is now heavily persecuted in mainland China where it has become too popular for a totalitarian power to tolerate.

The Mormon Church has had a history of making the establishment uncomfortable. Joseph Smith began receiving visits from the angel Moroni in upstate New York on September 21, 1823. The angel bore instructions from God that bade Smith to transcribe the religious history of an ancient American civilization, and in so doing, he created the Book of Mormon. According to this text the church set up by Jesus in Palestine had become corrupt, and the world had endured 1,500 years of apostasy as a result. It was up to Smith to restore the original Church of Christ.

As the church mushroomed in size it fled from western New York to Ohio, to Missouri, to Illinois, and eventually to the seclusion of Utah. Every move was necessitated by flared tensions. The Mormons directly inflamed the establishment by claiming the latter's version of Christianity was corrupt and had been for fifteen centuries. Mormon ideology was seen as pure heresy by their neighbors. These two factors, plus the very rapid growth of the new religion, proved to be such a threat to the status quo that it could not be tolerated.

Nauvoo, Illinois, was where the rapidly growing cult fled after the Missouri governor issued an order that Mormons must be "exterminated or expelled" (several Mormons were subsequently massacred following this order). The cult built a beautiful city that quickly prospered into the largest in Illinois. The cult thought that they had finally found their home.

However, just like the other places they had moved, tensions with neighbors grew. A paper that heavily criticized the Mormons was published and the Mormons fought back by destroying the paper's publishing facility. Joseph Smith was imprisoned and his guards stood by as an angry mob stormed the building and killed him. Smith's murder was almost the breaking point for the new religion.

After its leader's death, Brigham Young essentially saved the fledgling religion by literally removing it from a highly tense state. According to Jan Shipps, a Mormon scholar, when Young moved the Mormons to Salt Lake City, he "established such a firm boundary between the Saints and the non-Mormon world that the Saints in Utah were able to live outside the ordinary American political process."[2]

The Mormon Church had finally found a place where it could prosper and cement a community of devout followers. They were isolated from the anger of the American establishment. They were no longer existing in a state of high tension, and were able to lay the groundwork for what became exponential growth.

The Mormons' strategy is a drastic example of how to deescalate tension. But it saved the cult. Napster didn't fare so well. The new company was too offensive to the recording business, both in terms of jeopardizing its immediate bottom line, but more important, in terms of the long-term threat it posed to the very structure of the industry. So it persecuted them accordingly. Instead of retreating to live another day like the Mormons, Napster stood its ground and fought to the death.

Napster's Decline through the Eyes of an Apple

Napster's story is fairly well known. The brash music Internet company was founded by a college freshman named Shawn Fanning. He started it as a means to share rare songs with his friends, and it exploded into a full-scale cultural phenomenon. It did so many things right. Napster was an exemplary cult brand that enjoyed passionate consumer attachment even as it saw rapid growth. It demonized its opposition; it was a community built on customer interaction. But it failed at perhaps the most difficult aspect of cult brand formation—managing its tension. In effect, Napster was blinded by its own ideology and failed to realize that the institution that it was goading had the power to destroy it.

Napster grew at an almost unprecedented rate. Within Napster's first eighteen months, the service had grown from Shawn's thirty original friends to over eighty million users, each using the service to search for songs on Napster's central database and download them for free. By creating this enormous catalog of music (all the songs on each user's computer were in the database, literally billions of songs) that was so easy to access, young Mr. Fanning had managed to strike a chord that resonated with the millions of users who quickly joined Napster's ranks. Napster was about more than just free music; it was about freedom from the companies who wielded absolute control over that music the public could enjoy. With Napster, the common man was no longer dependent on the record labels for music—it was a new method of distribution.

Napster deliberately positioned itself as a leader of the new economic revolution that it had created. Using the Internet as his tool, Shawn Fanning had slapped the establishment in the face, showing that some punk programmer in jeans and a T-shirt could potentially take down an entire industry. John Perry Barlow noted in *Wired* magazine that this shift has been, "long awaited by some and a nasty surprise to others, the conflict between the industrial age and the virtual age is now being fought in earnest, thanks to that modestly conceived but paradigm shifting thing called Napster."

Napster consciously kept its tension with the recording industry high; it wanted friction to define itself as a freedom fighter versus the tyrannical bad guy. In the eyes of its members, music lovers' sovereignty was being squashed and pillaged by the totalitarian establishment who were forcing everyone to listen to Britney Spears and N'Sync. What really set Napster apart from the recording industry was that it didn't force anything on its users. Napster didn't try to influence users' preferences, and when you wanted a song, you got only that song and not fifteen other tracks that were undesirable (that you had to pay for). Napster users had ultimate control of their musical destiny.

But the record companies weren't only afraid that people were not buying as many CDs as in the past. (The entertainment industry as we know it is hurting. Since 2000, CD shipments are down 15 percent and 2002 was the first year that blank CD sales outnumbered sales for recorded CDs.) This shift in distribution methods, the companies realized, could render them extinct. In a virtual economy, music buyers could have a direct relationship with the producers and artists who distribute their songs through private web pages. If MP3s become the new medium of music dissemination, with their ease of transfer and use, CDs could easily become obsolete. It was clear that the record companies had to fight Napster for their own survival.

In December 1999 the Recording Industry Association of

America unleashed its ultimately fatal attack on Napster, suing them for copyright infringement. Expecting and wanting a fight, Napster and its supporters saw the battle as a David versus Goliath fight with their civil liberties at risk. How can you limit what people trade over the Internet? How is file sharing any different from burning a mix CD for your girlfriend, they raged? The RIAA, on the other hand, framed the battle as one of right versus wrong, painting Napster as a facilitator to robbery. Napster helped people steal from the record companies, and in turn, the artists themselves.

Eventually in 2001, the RIAA won, and a judge ordered Napster to shut down unless it could find a way to function within copyright laws. Napster's legal downfall came about because of how it operated through central servers that tracked and controlled the transfer of files between users. The judge saw Napster as an entity that acted as a distribution channel, therein, becoming more than just peers sharing files with each other.

Might things have happened differently if Napster had done a better job of handling its tension with the record industry? Quite possibly. Napster's successor Kazaa is profitable and has grown to be larger than Napster. According to industry leader, Download.com, Kazaa is the world's most downloaded software, with 230,309,616 downloads. To put that in perspective, a recent population estimate of the United States by the 2003 World Population Data Sheet came in at 291.5 million people. In many ways, Chris Sherman of *Online* was right when he said, "shuttering Napster will be like beheading Hydra, with two new heads growing back for every one hacked off."

Kazaa has learned from Napster's mistakes and is flourishing. While similar to Napster, Kazaa is a more legal beast. This is because Kazaa is completely decentralized and blind to the uses of its program. That is, Kazaa can't control what its users create and has no idea who is downloading what file, whether it is a copyrighted song or the directions to their boss's home. This decentralization begs the legal question: how can you be liable for illegal activity that you aren't aware of? Furthermore, according to Niklas Zennstrom, one of the two creators of Kazaa, the only way the system can be shut down is if every user elected to disable his program. So what is the point in persecuting something that is almost impossible to defeat?

The point is a simple and imperative one of survival. Kazaa poses an even greater threat to the establishment than Napster did because it allows for music, movies, games, pictures, and software to be shared between users.

Several recording labels and movie studios are currently suing Kazaa for copyright infringement, holding that Kazaa's creators knowingly created software that prevented them from having any control. Kazaa, taking Napster's freedom stance one step further, has filed a counter suit claiming that movie studios and recording labels don't understand the digital age and that when they act in concert, they have monopoly power in the distribution of entertainment.

However, Kazaa is doing things to balance its tension that Napster never did. Much like the Mormons, when the going got tough, Kazaa ran away. Kazaa was about to get an injunction in the Netherlands, where it was developed, so it sold its assets to a company in Australia which subsequently incorporated itself in Vanuatu, a tropical tax haven in the South Pacific with no copyright law. As such, it moved to a damper version of Utah, a haven from attack.

Kazaa also contends that its intent has always been to develop a means to distribute legal, copyrighted material. Nikki Hemming, CEO of Sharman Networks, which owns Kazaa, states that, "Our vision from inception was to develop and prove a model for the distribution of licensed content." And more important than its stated intent is the fact that Kazaa is developing channels that distribute licensed material. Kazaa is currently the world's largest distributor of licensed, digitally rights–managed content on the Internet, with more than 20 million licensed files downloaded per month. Through Kazaa's Altnet application,[3] users can download licensed material for as little as ten cents a song. Altnet is by no means floundering. It sells 500,000 licenses daily and since Sharman gets a cut of the sales, legal sharing could become its greatest source of revenue.

Even after the recording and movie companies sued Kazaa, Kazaa has been trying to establish a working relationship with them. According to Nikki Hemming, "The only thing preventing this product from being this amazing distribution mechanism is the lack of cooperation."

Signs of this cooperation are starting to appear. Recently, Sharman Networks launched a new version of Kazaa that expands the range of licensed content available to users with the addition of channels that allow users to search, browse, and buy content from third party providers. One of these channels is the Russell Simmons Hip-Hop channel, which will showcase short films from Def Filmmakers. This marks a significant step toward the establishment because Simmons is the founder of Def Jam Records, a very successful label.

In yet another sign of lessened tension with the establishment, Microsoft has chosen to distribute promotional trailers for the movie, *The Rules of Attraction*, in its Windows Media 9 format on Kazaa. The videos were put on the Kazaa network by Altnet, Kazaa's subsidiary that uses Microsoft's digital rights–management software to place electronic locks on the songs and videos it distributes. These locks deter unauthorized copying, enabling companies to take advantage of the virtually free distribution provided by Kazaa without losing the ability to demand payment and limit usage.

The entertainment industry is clearly up in arms over file sharing and in light of a federal ruling in 2003 that reinforced the legality of file sharing applications, it has decided to find other fish to fry—the users. The RIAA has decided that since it can't seem to shut down file sharing services like Kazaa, that it will sue the individual users of these services. In April of 2003, lawsuits were filed against students at Princeton, Michigan Technological University, and Rensselaer Polytechnic Institute that seek billions of dollars in damages—$150,000 per song. Additional suits were filed later in the year.

Not surprisingly, this move has failed to sit well with the public. Fred von Lohman, a lawyer for the Electronic Frontier Foundation, contends that, "This latest effort [by the RIAA] really indicates the recording industry has lost touch with reality completely. Today they have declared war on the American consumer."

While the entertainment industry is busy trying to sue individuals for using an application that has been judged to be within the bounds of legality, an old hat at cult formation has been scheming. Apple's Steve Jobs noticed something in Napster and Kazaa that reinforced his hypothesis: if file sharing is about the distribution of music and not free songs, then it should be possible to charge people to download music by the song.

Now, Apple isn't the first company to try and sell individual songs to users over the Internet, but it is the first to do so in a user-friendly environment that doesn't severely restrict ownership of the downloaded music. Apple's iTunes Music Store is as simple and intuitive as every other Apple product out there. You can listen to a thirty-second preview of any song and then buy it for ninety-nine cents with a click. There are no monthly subscription charges and you are actually buying the song instead of renting it compared to some of the other Internet music shops. The end product is even superior to the old MP3 format; songs will be encoded in a new ACC format that offers superior sound quality and smaller files. This means you can fit more, better quality music onto your iPod when you use iTunes.

Perhaps iTunes' best chance for success is that it has Steve Jobs as its leader. Sony's CEO, Andrew Lack, recalls, "I don't think it was more than a fifteen-second decision in my mind [to license music to Apple] once Steve started talking." Dr. Dre, an artist, producer, and one of the founding fathers of hip-hop, has noted that nobody has come up with a better plan to sell music online. In typical fashion, Jobs is not humble about his newest venture, claiming that his digital store will forever change the distribution of music, the marketing of the artists, and how the music is used by fans.

Napster and Kazaa demonstrated that the establishment had become outdated in its distribution model and that consumers felt marginalized by the monopolistic recording industries. Recognizing that the record labels are fighting for their lives, Jobs created a venture that is one notch closer to the establishment and therefore less tense than its predecessors. By signing on with Jobs, the recording industry is admitting that a new distribution system is needed, while maintaining its fight against the piracy of Kazaa. All that is left to see is whether the Napster catalyst really was about freedom of choice and not free music.

AN EARLY PRECEDENT

Interestingly, this case of Kazaa and Apple's iTunes learning from Napster's mismanagement of tension has a distinct parallel with the rise of Protestantism during the late Middle Ages. In the early fifteenth century, the Catholic Church had a monopoly over religion much as today's recording industry has a monopoly over the distribution of music. The Church consolidated its power by keeping all religious texts in Latin and making sure that its priests were the only ones who could read and interpret them for the general populace. God was not democratically distributed.

When the first religious reformers like Jan Hus of Bohemia began to call the Church's abuses of power to light, they were quickly killed off, much like Napster was. Hus was enraged by what he saw as an abuse of the Church's power with the selling of indulgences (essentially the sale of tickets to heaven) to finance a war between two papal claimants. Of course, the Church would not tolerate such a dissenting voice and burned Hus at the stake, showing the same sense of self-preservation that the RIAA employed in fighting Napster.

Hus's ideological successor, Martin Luther, followed a path more similar to Kazaa's or iTune's in his battle with the monolithic Catholic Church. He too, was angered by the selling of indulgences, this time to finance the building of St. Peter's Basilica in Rome. However, his tension with the establishment was significantly less than Hus's because German princes who were trying to wrest power away from the Church protected him. In effect, Luther had state sponsorship. The princes tempered Luther's tension with the Church, and with their protection he was able to nail his revolutionary Ninety-Five Theses on the doors of the cathedral in Wittenberg and start the Reformation.

With Luther's success Protestantism was born. The Catholic monopoly had been greatly weakened and the new Protestantism democratized religion to the point of preaching that everyone can commune with God.

Martin Luther and the more contemporary revolutionaries of Kazaa and iTunes have been successful because of their mediated tension with the establishment. While their ideas might have been born in the dying flames of their high-tension predecessors, they each placed themselves closer to societal norms in order to survive. They are different, but not too different.

Isolation: Too Much Tension Can Alienate Potential Customers

There is another possible fallout of too much tension, namely, that if you are too different you will alienate your cult's potential audience.

Cults are supposed to attract the alienated, not further alienate them. To be too deviant is to repel your potential recruits. If that happens, your cult or brand will be strangled by its lack of new membership, a noose of its own making.

The People's Temple is a particularly strong example of this self-strangulation. It was once a thriving cult. Their mass suicide at Jonestown was simply the final chapter of a decline that followed a period of rapid growth. In 1972, Jim Jones moved his cult, the People's Temple, to San Francisco where he hoped to be able to gather a greater following. Jones, a Christian minister with socially liberal views, had moved his organization twice before because of high tensions between it and the surrounding conservative communities.

San Francisco proved to be the perfect environment for the People's Temple to flourish because of its naturally liberal leanings and populace who felt alienated from the more conservative establishment. Soon its membership grew to over eight thousand people and Jones had become the toast of the city's liberal elite. Politicians courted Jones because of his unique ability to guarantee thousands of supporters and workers at rallies. Jones became a necessity at every major function in San Francisco. He was something of a religious celebrity.

However, during this time, Jones's beliefs became ever more deviant and an article in *New West* magazine exposed the San Francisco community to the true inner workings of the People's Temple. This article detailed fake healings, beatings, and other abuses, as well as the requirement that members liquidate their assets for the church. These reported events were the stimulus that eventually forced the People's Temple to leave San Francisco for Guyana.

Jones realized that with such bad press he would not be able to proselytize so effectively. Now, his deviance had been exposed, he faced the risk of not only stagnating, but also losing members because of their connections to the naysaying establishment. He knew that if he stayed in San Francisco the bad press would influence his existing members. He knew that estranged family members would crusade to win their children, brothers, and mothers back. He knew that he would lose many members to the palpable disdain of society. So he quickly mobilized as much of his group as he could, and retreated from establishment's scornful eye.

Deep in the jungle, Jonestown functioned outside of Guyanese society as a commune of foreigners who ignored their hosting government. Here, it was impossible for the cult to attract new members, Guyanese or American. But perhaps more importantly to Jones, it was also impossible for his members to defect. Their lives became completely dependent upon Jones and his community.

The People's Temple festered in the heat of Guyana until November 19, 1978. On that day they murdered a U.S. Congressman who had visited Jonestown to investigate allegations that Jones was keeping members against their will. Perhaps realizing that this heinous act effectively marked the end of his organization, Jones ordered the remaining nine hundred of his members to commit mass suicide by drinking cyanide-laced fruit punch. This drastic end to Jones's cult shocked the world.

As mentioned in the previous chapter, cults must make the novel familiar or they are doomed to be a flash in the pan. Too much deviance and they will wither and die. There are as many brand examples of these as there are cults. In fact they have come to define the term "cult brand" in many marketers' minds: niche, faddish, extreme, they disappear as fast as they arrive, because they mismanage tension.

One vivid example of this existed during the early 1990s in the United Kingdom. It was a brand of smokes called Death Cigarettes. Cigarettes labeling themselves "Death." Replete with the requisite skull and crossbones on its packaging and a label stating that tobacco seriously damages health? How cool! Finally a brand that mocked all the negative press about smoking. A brand that acknowledged that all smokers know that smoking is bad for them, but that they smoke anyway because they enjoy it.

Death Cigarettes quickly became the smoke of choice for all of London's many hipsters. But once their novelty wore off, Death Cigarettes quickly faded away because, well, people just don't like to be reminded of their mortality. Death Cigarettes' brand premise was just too different, too outside of what most people enjoy thinking about on a daily basis to become a long-term success.

Difference is a fickle beast. Cult leaders and brand managers must constantly monitor their organizations to make sure that their deviance is not enraging the establishment or offending potential members. But just as importantly, leaders must make sure that they are not becoming indistinguishable from their surroundings. Without difference, your cult won't act as a beacon to the dissatisfied and your existing members' passion will wane.

NOT ENOUGH TENSION

Snapple had managed to achieve a cultlike following by the early 1990s because of their stark difference from the rest of the beverage industry. It was quirky, from Brooklyn, and 100 percent natural, while their competitors were a spawn of faceless corporations. It was the perfect antagonist in the beverage industry and balanced an ideal amount of tension with its unique stance and communications.

Snapple's unusual advertising featured an actual employee named Wendy Kaufman, who quickly became known as the "Snapple Lady." Ms. Kaufman was the outgrowth of Snapple's desire to reflect their natural attributes with authentic advertising and she quickly became the brand's icon, differentiating Snapple from the other popular drink choices of Coke and Pepsi. And who would make a better icon than an "all natural," plump[4] employee whose job it was to answer Snapple fan mail? Their first ads featured the Snapple Lady sitting at her desk reading and answering actual letters from fans. Eventually, the campaign expanded to include Wendy fulfilling fan fantasies such as hosting a Snapple wedding.

Snapple's popularity grew with Wendy's and by the time Quaker Oats purchased Snapple for $1.7 billion, Snapple sales were approaching $700 million a year and Wendy was receiving up to 3,000 letters a week.[5] But Quaker decided to dump Wendy. They felt her thick Long Island accent was too regional and that the key to national success was to appeal to a broader audience.

Quaker obviously made the wrong choice. By dropping Ms. Kaufman and trying to appeal to everybody, they lessened Snapple's tension with the norm. Without Wendy, Snapple might was well be Coke or Pepsi, and Snapple's customer base was justifiably alienated from the brand. In just three years, and despite a $40 million sampling push, sales of Snapple plunged from a 1993 peak of 75 million cases to 45 million cases by 1996.[6]

By early 1997, a fan movement had begun to fight the corporate giant Quaker Oats to bring the Snapple Lady back.[7] Having learned a thing or two about marketing, Wendy helped snowball this movement by appearing on hundreds of radio shows that bashed Quaker Oats for killing *her* brand. One ardent fan built Ms. Kaufman a Web site to further her cause, and thus, www.snapplelady.com was born. Wendy's new Web site included a petition to get the Snapple Lady back and chat rooms where the community could meet and share Snapple-related stories. Soon, it started receiving thirty to forty thousand hits a week without any advertising—Snapple fans were finding their own ways to commune.

Later in 1997, Quaker decided to take a $1.4 billion loss and sold Snapple to Triarc Co. for $300 million. Triarc immediately decided to resurrect the Snapple Lady, and celebrated her return with a parade down Fifth Avenue that featured Ms. Kaufman clad in fruit and flowers on a palm tree–themed float, yelling, "I'm home. I'm back because they *need* me." Triarc explained Wendy's absence with a new commercial spot that explained that she had been on a two-year vacation on a remote island where the natives worship Snapple and released a limited-edition product called Wendy's Tropical Inspiration. The media loved this fanfare and Ms. Kaufman appeared on NBC's *Today Show*, ABC's *Regis & Kathie Lee*, and a host of other programs. And amazingly, within six months the sales decline was halted, a feat virtually unheard of in the world of beverage marketing.

Snapple was able to rewrite its history and reclaim its cult following simply by turning up the tension dial again. It created a huge business by maintaining enough tension with the norm. It was about being natural in a world of processed people and goods. Snapple was natural in its ingredients and natural in its business and communications. To drink Snapple was to be real, not some processed vessel of corporate will. Quaker Oats tried to make Snapple everyman's drink and failed. Once Triarc resurrected Snapple's deviance, its fans came running back.

Mass-cult brands are the arch manipulators of tension. They are able to artfully manipulate the tension dial to be *different enough*, but appear *similar enough*. A heavy hand can doom a cult. Too different and it alienates itself from its potential public, and invites its own destruction by an alarmed establishment. Too similar and it loses its reason for being to prospects and existing members alike. But just right, and it can thrive as a large and passionate community.

12

A CULT IS BORN

The jury is out on whether Saturn will remain a mass cult brand. Right now it is at a turning point. Which way the brand cult will move is unclear—will it become a regular car brand with some loyal customers, or an exceptional brand and corporate community with large degrees of loyalty and word of mouth? One of the most successful mass cult brands in history, Saturn stands to lose much because many of the essential founding elements of the cult have been dismantled or eroded over the past few years.

The Saturn story exhibits some of the most important ingredients for cult creation (the cult paradox, difference, making the novel familiar, power of the person, clear ideology, a sense of mutual responsibility, contact, and so on) which we will now review. It also displays some factors particular to the situation in which many managers of large corporations find themselves.

Saturn was formed because of the threat of superior competition that was nimbler, smarter, and offered cheaper and better products than GM could deliver. GM was being crucified in the small car segment by the Japanese car industry. Starting in the seventies, the car giant had tried several strategies to repulse the threat. It launched its own response, the Chevette. It tried to buy equity stakes in Isuzu and Suzuki (if you can't beat them join them). It tried a joint venture with Toyota. None of these classic strategies really addressed the issue however. The problem was not just the competition; it was the industry itself. The competition had simply highlighted that the American car industry was fundamentally flawed. Its own inherent failings simply left it vulnerable to newer and better ideas.

How was the industry flawed? It had a systemic failure. The leadership at GM and the UAW both agreed that every "given" in their industry was hobbling competitiveness, especially the poisonous relationship between the two organizations. They agreed that the issue had become so acute that it was in everyone's interest for something new to be tried.

Up to that point, each side had tried their own classic territorial maneuvers. The management solution to noncompetitive pricing was to turn up the speed dial of the assembly line—brute-forcing productivity. The attempt to buy stakes in Japanese companies and brand their imported models was also a strategy to bypass the union. In the face of job losses, the union made it more painful to shed jobs with costly strikes. In a depressing cycle of predictable, shortsighted strategies, the competitive threat was made more potent not by anything the Japanese were doing, but by the instinctive response of an industry atrophied by convention.

The "99"

In 1983 fifty people from the UAW, and fifty from GM management (one of the 100 eventually left, and so they became the legendary "99") formed a study group to examine the industry. Not only did they find out how the Japanese did what they did, but how the American car industry had done what it had done—how it had ended up in such a mess. They traveled the world touring companies that exhibited best practice both within and without their industry.

Within a year the team concluded that the most productive organizations focused on people, systems, and cooperation. The 99 was, in fact, a living embodiment of their own recommendations. GM must change by creating an ethos of cooperation and convention-challenging. The genesis of Saturn was founded not in the idea to launch a new, more competitive brand, but in labor relations.

Fine, but if the idea was to create an organization where management and union worked together and where new processes were implemented, what form would it take and what would it produce? Should these new practices be tried at an existing plant? No, too much, too soon. This radical experiment could dangerously destabilize a huge organization. At the same time that these issues were being considered, the superior Japanese models were forcing GM to recognize that their product was flawed. They needed a good quality small car that competed with its foreign challengers.

In 1984, a small group at GM, including CEO Roger Smith, concluded that the right thing to do was to make this entity a completely separate venture. Don Hudler, former CEO of Saturn, said it "was a venture between the UAW and GM to see how small car manufacturing could be kept in the U.S." That it became a whole new subsidiary, a new brand, with a designed-from-scratch new car and a radical new retail system took most of the industry by surprise, including many at GM. Joe Kennedy, former head of Sales and Marketing, says this decision was made with no study and very little consultation. It was an impulse decision. No one even bothered to do the normal legal trademark checks on the name. Nonetheless, the new company was announced in the first week of January 1985.

Roger Smith spawned what could in effect appear to be a direct challenge to the core business. He chose to launch a new company with totally new practices, with the mandate to challenge every-thing, and to launch a new product, brand, and distribution chan-nel. He was either building a folly that would swallow a huge investment, or he was launching a competitor to his own business.

He realized that heretical ideas would be suffocated in the stale air of convention. To escape the poisonous legacy of the establish-ment he really had no choice but to take a gamble. The only chance that heretical ideas had of making it would be in a greenfield site, literally. In a state far away from the smokestacks of Detroit and the cynical eye of management and worker, Saturn was built in a bu-colic setting near the town of Springhill, Tennessee.

An established institution spawning its own cult had been tried before. The Catholic Church between the fourteenth and seven-teenth centuries faced thousands of challengers that were stealing millions of its members. It had attempted to become the Universal Church, to be market dominant, to be the only candidate for reli-gious expression. In the attempt to appeal to all it had become indi-visible from the state as a governing institution. It often appeared more worldly than its secular partner. Calls for a return to the fun-damentals of Christianity were legion. Cults and sects were crop-ping up everywhere (Martin Luther was but one of many hundreds of dissenters over several generations) and gaining significant con-gregations of passionate followers. Old ideas appeared bankrupt and irrelevant to a population demanding more genuine spiritual satisfaction. The church was at the top of its S-curve. It had to do something radical to satisfy the radicalism of the age.

In a brilliant move to out-compete its competitors, it "culted" it-self. Church leaders created the monastic orders of Cistercians and Dominicans, aesthetic communities that attracted passionate ad-herents who might well have gone to the myriad competitive cults and sects to satisfy their need for spiritual fulfillment. For several centuries they thrived as places where vigorous theology existed outside the corrupting influence of the main body of the church, and to a significant degree, was successful in defusing the potential of its competitors.

A sponsored cult can of course be allowed to succeed to the point where it seriously challenges the survival of the parent. It can be nurtured to become the new iteration of the mother organization and eventually grow to replace it—a more vigorous, more relevant, more innovative child of an aging parent. The Catholic Church chose not to let this happen. They used the monastic orders as homes for their own discontents lurking within the main body of the church, and as an option for outsiders tempted by competitive offerings. But they did not let the new orders grow to become challengers to the established Church's hegemony (something we'll see echoed in GM's ultimate strategy with regard to Saturn).

Start a Cult with Heretics

The 99 made their recommendations. Smith made the decision to create a separate company. Now they had to find the people to run it. This was 1985, five years before launch. Not only would the venture require the special kind of people that could launch the first new car company in America in fifty years, design and produce a new brand, and establish a new distribution network. But it also demanded the kind of people who could stomach generating and implementing ideas that flew in the face of virtually every convention in the car industry. It was a "brave and crazy risk," as the ranks of GM saw it.

These individuals would face pressure from their own demons of doubt tutored by years of immersion in one of the most hidebound industries. They would face derision from the rest of the industry. They would perhaps face pressure from their own compatriots in mainstream GM management and the UAW who would conceivably see them as recklessly destabilizing a delicately constructed status quo. But perhaps equally seriously, they would have to give up the familiar and take a risk. For many, the opportunity cost was too high.

You might expect that the entire 99 were obvious and immediate recruits for the embryonic company. They were the ones that had undertaken the study, knew the serious flaws of the status quo, and had ideas on how to fix them. They knew the devil, and it wasn't better than the alternative. Yet only twenty or so of the original group migrated into Saturn. As Joe Kennedy put it: "Some of them were traditional union guys, or traditional management guys who came together to do a study, but couldn't see letting go of the world as they knew it. They may have intellectually understood the concepts that they discovered, but they couldn't emotionally."

The founders self-selected on the basis of comfort with heresy and passion for the idea. Joe described these early members as "closet heretics." By inclination they would question anything, and now they were given the opportunity to follow through. The gate through which the founders had to pass was one of cost: "You could not join Saturn lightly." To commit to something you must give up something valuable, in this case a cushy job and predictable outcomes, an easier task for those heretical by nature.

The Cult Paradox in Action at Saturn

The closet heretics that lurked at the margins of GM were identified and brought into a community where a culture of respect and what Joe calls "giving people the appropriate dignity" gave them confidence to voice their crazy ideas.

It was safe enough for grown men to feel comfortable coming to tears over some issues. Joe expressed it as a highly creative community where everyone was "living on the high wire of emotion." Factory workers, management suits, and salty union negotiators were not the kind of people you'd expect to "let loose with some deeply personal story or angle that brings a level of power to an idea," but they could at Saturn.

What made the Saturn community especially close was an accumulation of a classic set of community building circumstances. There was a clear threat: the Japanese invasion that was jeopardizing jobs. It was fueled by the awareness that everyone had made some sacrifice to be there. It had a clear ideology, one of respect or "humanity" as Joe called it. The members did not really feel comfortable, fulfilled, or recognized elsewhere in the GM organization. "High contact" was forced between members. Saturn ran offsite courses that forced intimacy and trust amongst all the players that included a famous climbing wall (the program was called "learning the ropes"). Over fifteen thousand people went through the program. This tight community of misfits enabled the paradox to work. "People were able to blossom who might not have been envisioned as blossoming in another context . . . people became very successful [at Saturn] who were either not, or could not be envisioned, as successful in the GM or UAW context." In other words, they became more themselves.

The Holy Trinity

At Saturn, the community was a Holy Trinity. The plant, the retailers, and the customers all developed strong communities among themselves. But the real community lay within the sense of responsibility that they had *for each other.* At all points of contact, for any of the stakeholders, the experience was one of belonging to a community of mutual responsibility between makers, sellers, and buyers.

Don Hudler emphasized that, "Well, we realized we needed each other." What initially started as what he called a "partnership" between the UAW and management evolved into one with "the retailers, which evolved into one with the customers . . . and they would help us sell cars." The end benefit of advocacy was a function to a large degree of the sense of responsibility the customer had to the Saturn Family. Many groups traditionally alienated by the car industry (women, young buyers, ethnic groups, and homosexuals) became disproportionately represented within the Saturn buying population. Suzanne, a woman in her mid-twenties who worked in the media said, a little embarrassed, "I felt stupid buying into the whole Saturn Family thing, but I just bought in so hard . . . they were going to be a different kind of company." She recommended the brand to at least twenty of her friends and colleagues.

A Cause

The power of a cause—to fight an enemy, to right a wrong, to implement a better way—is to unify and galvanize members to action behind a common goal. The ostensible cause for Saturn appeared to be the critical need to face off a threat. The Japanese were coming and it was down to this team to save the day and faith in the American car industry. The brand name is a legacy of this original goal. It does not refer to the heavenly body in our solar system as most believe (and the logo subsequently was designed to recall). It was called the Saturn project after the space program that was started in the sixties. The NASA program was designed to catch up and overtake Russia's surprise and humiliating lead in the space race. GM's Saturn project was founded as an attempt to redress the shaming of the American car industry by the Japanese.

This may have been the stimulus for the project, but is what not what became the true cause for the Saturn creators. It was not rich and sustainable enough. It was an external stimulus, one that might eventually go away. For the passionate heretics, the cause evolved from repulsing a threat, a cause based on fear, to changing the world for the better, one based on righteousness. It was an internal motivating force that infused the cause with the energy it needed to fight the real enemy, the status quo. The status quo abused everyone: customers, workers, and management. It must be overturned.

The operating idea of the founders was "if we always do what we've always done, we'll always get what we've always got." This attitude generated what became the core ideology of the organization that fueled the cause. It's not written down anywhere, but its genesis was embedded in the recommendations of the 99: *respect for each other.* As Don Hudler remembers, "The premise was that whatever it is people are doing, most of them already have most of the answers figured out ... we listened to people whether they were production workers, potential customers, or whether they were Saturn retailers." That is how innovations such as the car clinics, that became a defining idea for the brand, were adopted and flourished.

Interestingly, the ideology of respect flowed from the internal community to the external customer community. With most companies this flows in reverse order. When a company discovers the power of treating its customers well, it generally translates that practice internally, transforming everyone inside into a customer. At Saturn the ideology flowed all the more powerfully from inside the organization to the outside. The customer was buying into a core belief and practice already present within the company and as such it felt all the more genuine.

Customers Rooting for the Cause

If the status quo is something generally believed to be bankrupt, the ideology of a cult can become adopted by the disenfranchised and elevated into a cause. Something of this nature happened to Saturn. The extension of the cause to the customer base happened because they could identify with it. At one level, Saturn was fixing a problem that no one else had the courage or desire to address (a retail experience that normally felt like root canal treatment).

At a whole other level, customers were buying into respect as a larger idea. Respect was missing in the service business generally. But it was also missing in everyday life for many of Saturn's customers. As Joe says, "I think the people that Saturn serves are ordinary people. We didn't serve the rich, we didn't serve the upscale, we served a lot of 'heart of America' kind of people." The respect with which they were treated in the dealership resonated, and the stories they saw in the commercials featuring customers like them being respected struck a cord. As Joe says "they, too, were regular employees in big corporations that didn't listen to their employees and didn't involve them in decisions. And hey, here's this company doing all these neat things. And I know it's real because I've been through the experience of buying one and I've felt it."

They were rooting for an idea. And rooting for an idea makes money. I asked why Suzanne bought Saturns: "The car was nice enough looking and I needed an economical car. But I like the idea of the company . . . I really went because of the message . . . it's sort of a democratic car, a Midwestern car . . . full of substance." She was again embarrassed that she was buying into the thing wholesale for such an advertising literate, cynical individual. But as she said, "They were a total package of, like, ideology . . . you think you're immune, and here I am thinking about it again . . . I'm excited."

Commitment

Be authentic. Joe Kennedy agreed that the cult only works if the customer feels a genuine commitment. He related how he has other companies coming to him to ask what they should do to imitate Saturn's success: "Someone would say 'Teach me how to get this cultlike enthusiasm for my product.' And we'd say, 'Well, what do you believe in?' And they would say, 'We'll believe in whatever we need to believe in to do it.' And we'd say, 'Well if that's your attitude, you'll never do it.' "

One of the secrets behind the success of the Saturn cult was that it wasn't a lie. The ideology of respect was so vigorously held within the internal community that it ensured that the customer experience was real. Don Hudler knew from the outset that it was the retail network that would be the brand to a major degree. Wayne, another loyal customer said he bought the car because of the customer experience: "They treat you with respect." Despite the fact that his most recent purchase was "a little more expensive than some of the others (he also comparison-shopped Honda and Toyota)" he bought Saturn because "they're really working for you . . . so it's like we're all a big Saturn Family. So it's like you're hanging out with people like you. You're going to see your family. That's kind of their mantra." These are also the words of a member of a marketing-literate generation. Wayne is a ponytailed, earringed family man in his late twenties working as a hardware and software buyer for a midsized company, pretty self-aware and acutely attuned to what he calls "marketing-bullshit." You cannot get this kind of sustained buy-in if there is a whiff of inauthenticity.

Cults Start from Within

How do you ensure authenticity? The most effective way is to ensure that there is a cult within the organization, not just among its members. The clergy must be as committed as the congregation. Constructing a cult following a formula can be done, but is a dangerous game; any hint of hypocrisy can be its undoing (the Catholic Church is having a challenging time right now). All those who worked at the Saturn plant and the retailers were chosen, or self-selected on the basis of their passion for the idea, or they were closet heretics seeking a better "church" in which to practice. They all had sacrificed something to join. The management and line workers alike had lost seniority and taken a cut in pay to enlist. Retailers were making a financial investment in an idea that most of the industry thought was lunatic and doomed to failure.

The internal passion was cultlike and translated palpably to the external followers. The plant, retailers, and customers alike all bought into the vision. More than that, they all had a sense of belonging to something different, where divisions between management, production line, customer, and retail network were truly obscured.

And it worked. Don Hudler says that the original business goal for the addition of Saturn to the GM line-up was a net 75 percent more sales from customers that would have otherwise gone to competitive brands. This it achieved in its early days, and continues to do now. In addition, it reinvented how cars are sold in America. No small feat for a low price car company that to this day beats luxury brands in terms of customer experience.

13

THE CULT WAVERS, A CHURCH STRENGTHENS

For all its early success, the future of Saturn as a mass cult brand is unsure. Its initial meteoric rise on the automotive scene has slowed, and in recent years production lines have been down as new models have been introduced but not met sales expectations. And many of the founders of the cult have left.

Saturn is showing some of the classic signs of self-destruction seen in cults throughout history thanks to three of the classic cult "destroyers": a lack of perceived mutual investment, a decline of the internal cult that sustained the distinctive ideology, and too much tension.

On the other hand, some of the basics of a car brand have been improved. Saturn has finally become more than a one-car company with the introduction of a midsize model and an SUV. The cult appears to be alive and well at the most important point of contact with the customer: the retailer network. And finally, the mother church has itself become more effective by adopting some of Saturn's practices and its personnel (the two are connected).

So which way will it go? Let's look at these more recent events in a little more detail.

Lack of Mutual Investment

By the time the brand was three or four years old, the company's financial commitment was looking a little thin from the consumers' perspective. The car was never intended to be an engineering breakthrough. It was to be competitive with the very good Japanese small car market, and it was, offering good value for money in terms of reliability, safety, and basic specs. But it was beginning to be left behind and it was looking a little old. What's more, those loyal to the Saturn brand who wanted to trade up couldn't. It was a one-car brand. Don Hudler said, "we were losing customers who wanted to stay with Saturn, but we didn't have the products that met their needs." It was "like having a Civic or Corolla franchise."

Customers were right in thinking that the company was hedging its investment in them. For a new model to be in the showrooms three years after the brand's launch, the go-ahead on the midsize car would have had to be signed off at the launch. It was 1991 and GM was going through a particularly tough time. It had "other mouths to feed" in terms of the other brands, according to Hudler, and they had to cut somewhere. There was the argument—with which Hudler sympathized—that before Saturn was given another billion dollars, it should show a return on the $2 billion already invested.

By the end of the decade, Saturn customers' loyalty was being stretched. The experience in the store was still beyond compare, especially in the low priced sector, but it was, at the end of the day, a car company and the cars were not up to par.

Too Much Tension

Tension started to dial up dangerously at Saturn in the late nineties during an especially bitter dispute between the GM and the UAW union. The heads of the respective sides called in the loyalties of their members at Saturn who, until then, had been protected from what had become an even more poisonous relationship at the head office. Saturn needed production at the GM plants maintained so that it could continue to use their parts to build its cars irrespective of any dispute in Detroit. This was seen as a violation of loyalties by both the main management and union. No longer would both sides at headquarters treat Saturn as an exception. Its special status within GM was eroded and both Saturn management and union representatives were ordered to toe the line with their respective organizations.

What's more, leadership within GM changed and proffered a new strategy. Commonality was the theme: bring structures and processes in line within the corporation. This made business sense. Economies of scale were needed to make GM more competitive. But it flew in the face of the founding notion of Roger Smith. He knew that Saturn's radicalism would only work if it was kept at arm's length from GM headquarters. It had a separate plant, its own processes, and its own unique culture.

Saturn produced only 3 to 4 percent of GM's sales, but it had a much higher percentage of mind-share within the organization. As such it attracted much resentment. It was viewed as "the late child in a wealthy family." There were jealousies. Saturn and its children "were spoiled, given everything that the older kids had to work their asses off for," says Don Hudler.

This was a case of a business unit entering too high a state of tension *with its own holding company.* The child was upsetting the parent.

The Vatican Absorbs Its Own Cult

GM brought Saturn within the walls of the mother church. Roger Smith had maintained Saturn's distance by allowing the new division to report directly to the president of GM, Lloyd Reuss. Skip Lafauve, the original CEO of Saturn, Hudler (who replaced him when Lafauve retired), and other senior managers at Saturn would travel to Detroit every month to update Reuss on their progress and plans. All the other divisions of GM, immense in their own right, had to report to one of the many vice presidents. Saturn's unique reporting structure has been dismantled and it has now fallen in line with usual practice at GM.

Saturns are now designed at GM's main design facility. It shares many basic parts with other divisions. The cars are also now made at other plants. The midsized car was the first to be built outside of Springhill in Wilmington, Delaware, by plant workers who had none of the Saturn cultural legacy. Many within the industry blame these moves for a decline in the quality of the product.

The Internal Cult Dies

Skip Lafauve, a quietly charismatic man and the leader of Saturn, retired. "He wasn't a song-and-dance man . . . he got people excited because of his compassion and his own commitment to what he was doing," said Hudler. The union leader at the Saturn plant, Michael Bennett,[1] was ousted. Other founding leaders left Saturn and were brought into roles within GM. Michael Bennett complained that it's "the entire dismantling of the entire Saturn concept—it's no longer a different kind of car company, and it's no longer a different kind of car."[2]

When I asked Hudler whether there is the same degree of ownership and mutual responsibility amongst the Springhill members that had been Saturn's defining idea, he admitted "it exists to a lesser degree . . . although there's some people that still cling to it."

He also confessed that the early zealotry had eroded. Why? "You don't have the freshness that once gave us all the more energy," he said. It's harder to keep things going than it is to start something new. (He has retired from Saturn management and opened his own Saturn chain of retail outlets in Texas.)

Not all is gloomy for Saturn, far from it. The products themselves are more plentiful and produced at competitive costs by amortizing resources with GM. Although profitability had never been the prime objective for the Saturn launch (stemming the loss and recapturing customers in the small car segment had been the goal, which it achieved handsomely), profitability is projected to reach acceptable standards. There has also been a less tangible but arguably more impactful effect of the integration of Saturn.

Absorption of Your Own Cult Can Be a Sound Strategy

The mother church has improved its own effectiveness by embracing its own difficult child. Two or three hundred key people from Saturn were absorbed into GM at senior levels. Six of the eleven top Saturn management became officers at the mother church replacing their responsibilities at the smaller company for the equivalent, but much larger ones at the parent. As a result "a lot of the things we did at Saturn are now standard at GM," Don claims proudly, although he was hesitant to go on because "people at GM bridle at this . . . they get very upset that this upstart could teach them anything."

Absorbing the upstart is a sound strategy if your long-term objective is to create innovation at the main institution. It permits revolution with low risk. Heretics and their ideas were greenhoused at Saturn. Upsetting the status quo was limited within the confines of a relatively small province of GM until the innovations were proven in the marketplace. The best ideas were reintegrated, the resisters of change at GM were gagged by the undeniable evidence of dramatic business results. The company got a revolution without upsetting the apple cart. What's more, as Roger Smith wisely noted, there was no massive institution to stifle the ideas. Spawning them outside in a greenfield site, and then integrating the ones that worked inside was a sound strategy.

However, you can only do this once. GM has risked the erosion of the all that makes Saturn a good car division by drawing it within the purview of the establishment. Once the cult is in, it's in. You will be very lucky if you can maintain heresy if you have absorbed the leaders into the mother church, and pulled the amputated cult within controlling distance.

The Cult Lives on—Outside the Mother Church

Actually, GM has been able to draw in the cult *and* maintain some of its cultlike quality. The cult appears to be alive and well in the remote reaches of the satellite churches of Saturn—the retail network. Saturn's heresy was truly manifested to the consumer at the point of sale. It was the reason the majority of them bought the car, again and again, and why they recommended it, again and again.

The retail experience was radical. Many others have since copied it, but few have really reproduced the experience. Some have stolen the idea of no-haggle pricing. Others have redesigned their show-rooms to feel more user-friendly and less like storage facilities with men in bad suits. But few have really got to the heart of what made the experience different, the people. Saturn hired virgins, those who had never been tainted by the sleazy deal, and refugees, those who wished to escape from it. Saturn retailers would "rather them not have experience," Bob Abernathy, a leading car retail manager in Texas told me. "We don't want bad habits . . . inexperience we're happy with. We would rather train them ourselves."

Does the zealotry and vision still exist amongst the staff? Does the customer still feel the difference and believe that the famed Saturn Family still exists? I visited a retail outlet and spoke to the staff, and interviewed some customers who had recently bought Saturns.

The dealership I visited doesn't really feel like one. It's small, in-timate, and homey. Almost immediately upon entering you find yourself facing a reception desk with a friendly young man waiting behind it. Behind him is what looks like someone's living room with comfortable club chairs, a carpet, magazines, and doughnuts and coffee. There were no seedy little offices with dealers hunched over papers talking conspiratorially to nervous looking customers about the special deal he's negotiated with his boss just for them. There were "guest areas" (you are a guest before you buy a car, a customer after you've joined the family) consisting of wooden ta-bles and chairs in the open ("there's nothing to hide . . . all the prices are the same for each customer") with consultants in open necked sports shirts chatting to relaxed families.

Bob showed me the "launch bay" where customers receive their new car, are introduced to the whole team (whatever employee is around, whether mechanic or service manager or porter), and shout the Saturn cheer: "We say, We say, Saturn!" He showed me the consultants' shared office where they call a customer the day after delivery and again three days after to check whether they are happy with their purchase. I asked him whether the car clinics and barbecues still happen. The clinics are run quarterly and barbecues are held by each store "on a whim," maybe once a month or every two months.

How does the staff feel about the brand and their jobs? I spoke to the service manager who had been at the store in its former location for ten years. His job was to organize the service, of course. But he said his real job was to "make the marriage work" through the frequent contact of the servicing experience. The sales consultants do the "ceremony and the honeymoon." As a result, he estimates that the outlet gets roughly a 70 percent recommendation rate from existing customers.

Abernathy believes that the Saturn Family, although it sounds corny, is real. He claims, "If you broke down in Houston with a normal car, no one would pull over unless to rob you. If you are driving a Saturn, another customer would pull over and help." He introduced me to Art, who four years ago was a virgin. Prior to becoming a sales consultant he was a professional photographer. Instead of a job offered to him at a local university, he took one at Saturn instead, but not before he interviewed other consultants at associated outlets to check on the veracity of the claims about the culture. A stocky, muscular man with a short beard and engaging talkative manner, he enjoys working there "because of the camaraderie." He claims that the culture of respect is alive and well and that "we treat each other the same way we treat our customers." I asked him where that comes from. He said bad sales consultants self-eject: "I think the kind of people that end up staying are the right kind of people. We're basically nice. The others just spin off."

Do the customers feel it? Art, of course, claims that they do. He says that at bottom it's the service they get: "these people come back to Saturn for maintenance when they could go to Jiffy Lube or their neighborhood mechanic. It is, that's the joke, you know, the Saturn

Family, but it's true. I mean, it's almost like becoming a member of a club."

To check I interviewed a few customers at the other end of the country. Wayne had just bought a Saturn in upstate New York replacing one he had for ten years. Why another Saturn? "We bought it because we like the brand." What was the brand as far as he was concerned? "The dealer experience." They had been going to various Saturn dealerships for servicing of their previous car for ten years. Interestingly, when they went to a dealer in Westchester to buy their second car, the experience was not good. Wayne shook his head and said "it was just awful." He kept going back refusing to believe his beloved brand could be like that: "maybe they were having an off day," but they were "just not nice people." Did this put him off? Thankfully for Saturn, he rationalized it as not "Saturn-like" (coincidentally a term used internally by the original founders). He wrote it off as an exception.

He found a place that was more typical in his view. The personnel were "more casual" than the Honda dealership he had also tried when he comparison shopped. At Honda he encountered "prototypical pushy salesmen." It wasn't a high-pressure sale at Saturn—"He didn't try to sell me on the extras; in fact, I had to ask him 'what are the extras?' "

The numbers seem to prove the point that the cult is still working at point of sale. Last year Saturn got best overall rating by J.D. Powers for service excellence, and was beaten this year only by luxury brands. But what about that poor dealership that Wayne found? The rigorous vetting of retailers that had occurred at Saturn's foundation no longer takes place, according to Hudler. Clearly it needs to be reinstituted as new customers come to the brand. They are unlikely to be as charitable as Wayne.

The cult is alive and well at the retailer level, apart from this worrying aberration in Westchester. The employees have still got religion and so has the customer. But there is a lurking threat to this satellite cult. GM must resist the temptation to bring the retail organization under closer control. According to Hudler, the marketing and retail relationships to date are essentially unchanged in their separation from the mother church. However, this year the Saturn retailers' annual meeting was integrated into the larger GM bash. At one point the Saturn retailers entered a room for a cocktail party with "five thousand of their closest friends." Don says: "They really didn't like it . . . because of the loss of camaraderie." Mortified at the turn of events, the Saturn dealers insisted "overwhelmingly that 'we need to have a Saturn-only thing' " next year.

Not giving them their own annual meeting was clearly a mistake and if it's not a one off, the internal cult amongst this unique network will die—and with it the experience that sells the car. The Saturn Family is palpably felt by retail employees and customers alike must be maintained. If the internal cult at the retail level is extinguished by not keeping it separate from mainstream GM, then the external cult will also fail. As long as the customer feels the authenticity of the cult at the retailer level, then its death at the plant may have less of an impact.

The Long View: The Mother Church Adopted an Effective Defense

During the course of this book we've examined how brand cults are made. We've looked at things from the perspective of organizations that are often the *challenger* of the status quo. But what if your organization is the one being *challenged?* What if in your market, new ideas have emerged and are gaining popular and passionate support? Roger Smith was facing this scary predicament in the early eighties. The Japanese car makers were the heretical organisms that had entered the U.S. market and were stealing away a significant congregation. If you face this problem (it is at some point inevitable for any dominant entity) then the following strategies may help. GM, the challenged incumbent, ultimately used two of the strategies with its launch and reintegration of Saturn.

THREE STRATEGIES TO DEAL WITH COMPETITORS' CULTS

These three options, used in the past by threatened churches, and today by threatened corporations and brands, are open to you as potential defenses against competitive heresy. Only two of them are real defenses, however, because only two yield sustainable answers.

1. Persecution

Pour resources and energy into destroying dangerously heretical organizations. Persecution has been the consigliere of organized religion for millennia as a way as staving off competitors. But business has not escaped the temptation to brutalize competitors, either. For example, the major airlines' automatic response to fledgling competitors has been to overwhelm them with scheduling and undercut them with unsustainable pricing. (Swallowing this cost is seen as a sound investment to drive the upstart into oblivion.)

This is only a short-term solution. If the dominant incumbent is really bankrupt and irrelevant then heresy will prevail. You may be able to kill off one cult, but another will surely emerge to satisfy the latent needs of a dissatisfied consumer population or congregation. Although they stamped out calls for reformation for centuries, the Catholic Church ultimately could not prevent it.

2. Absorption

Absorbing competitive ideas into your own organization has also been a tactic used for thousands of years. Much of what is now believed to be its own unique theology the Christian Church actually stole from competitive cults. It essentially defused the challengers' power by co-opting their difference. (GM's attempt to buy into its Japanese competitors could be seen as such a strategy.) This can be a very successful long-term strategy. It can produce its own problems, of course, typical of many attempts to merge organizations with different cultures.

3. Culting Yourself

Saturn is a good example. Culting yourself can be a very smart way of repulsing others by beating them at their own game. The idea is to launch your own cult. Establish a separate entity with its own theology and devoted followers, and invest in it so that it steals share from the newcomers. Protect yourself by attacking like with like.

This last strategy worked for ten years. Then GM pulled Saturn closer to the mother church in terms of reporting structure and control of its processes and output. But it also employed the second strategy outlined above. It absorbed the heretics and their theology into the main church and became the stronger for it. GM actually exploited both strategies—absorption and self-culting. In effect, it had two bites at heresy—by starting its own cult, and then absorbing its fledgling into the main body of the company and rein-venting itself from within.

The original Saturn founders may look on sadly as the cult of Springhill declines, but the larger picture for GM could well have improved. As long as it can maintain the cult at the retailer and cus-tomer level, then it may be able to have it both ways—to reinvent itself from within *and* have a thriving cult.

14
WHO RUNS THE CULT?

"**P**ower-crazed control freaks" would be the verdict of most people. Informed by images of Applewhite, Jim Jones, and Koresh, whose whims dictated the very existence of their followers, the average person quite reasonably concludes that a mandate to wield absolute power defines a cult leader.

Actually, the most successful cults have quickly distributed power and responsibility beyond the founder or one central figure. There is one fundamental flaw that puts severe limits on the longevity of a despot's cult: the despot's own longevity. Cult leaders tend to die. Proxies can be built into the organization to perpetuate a founder's role (as have the Catholics, in the form of the Pope, or the Mormons in the form of the Living Prophet; in these cases the God-given mandate for revelation and control is passed from one leader to the next). Otherwise ownership of the organization must be shared more widely within the franchise for the cult to live beyond a human lifespan.

"Command-Control" is not a sustainable model for brands in contemporary marketing either. Of course brand managers have never had the power of a despot. But the organizational model they work within is an attempt at direct manipulation of customer behavior from one central point. For the past fifty years or so most companies have followed the paradigm institutionalized by Procter and Gamble. The brand manager is, as they call it, "the General Manager of the brand." They are the commanders who dictate what the product, packaging, advertising, promotion, pricing, distribution, and budget will be. Into the market goes the brand shaped by these decisions. And especially during the fifties and sixties when this model first came into its own, consumer behavior jerked with almost puppetlike responsiveness to the brand manager's will. It was an era when the producer, not the consumer, dictated the terms.

But this model has become old. Even within the world of *cult* brands where extreme attachment is expected, the old command control method of management is increasingly rare. Ownership of the brand must be shared with its membership for it to thrive. The power has shifted. The new protagonists are the consumers and they are demanding a greater role in the shaping of their own community. This is to be encouraged of course. A feeling of ownership will normally lead to feelings of loyalty to the community they've helped shape.

But that redefines the role of a brand manager. For a cult brand, his or her role in this consumer society is *less* one of a *commander* of the market place, and *more* of a *supporter and nurturer* of the community their brand may be fortunate enough to enjoy. But that demands a massive change of attitude. The vocabulary that's still used today in the marketing world is telling. It's drawn from the command-control culture that it's imitated for generations: that of the military. Marketers run "campaigns," they "target" consumers, they go for "market domination," they "launch" an "attack" on competitors, they "penetrate" markets, and "capture" market share.

The following are some models that portend the future. They all distribute responsibility for the running of cult, some much more than others. And imbedded in them all is *respect* for the role of the community.

All this is not to say that there is no role for a "charasmatic leader." If you have one, use them. Steve Jobs, Malcolm Forbes, Mary Kay have all been huge assets to their brands. As we have seen, they can become metaphors for the members of the community, and often write the founding ideology. But it is very important to ensure that their power is distributed before their disappearance predicts that of the cult brand. Any good manager knows that absolute power in the hands of one person, no matter how effective they may be, yields only a short-term benefit to the organization.

The Member as Priest Model

This model provides for a certain amount of direction from above, but with a sense of ownership and accountability throughout. As such, its membership tends to be highly loyal, extremely motivated, and very energetic on behalf of the organization. Not surprisingly, some of the organizations that we have spent the most time talking about in this book are the ones that live this model.

The structure of the Mormon Church is very rigid, apparently onerously hierarchical, and seemingly all power is vested at its peak. At the top there is a Living Prophet. Beneath him are two counselors. Together with the quorum of twelve apostles directly underneath them on the organizational chart, this select fifteen are responsible for making and maintaining official church policy. Beneath the quorum of apostles there are seventy area presidents with each area president being responsible for several stakes. Each stake is made up of several wards and every ward has a bishop who is responsible for a local congregation.

To reinforce the apparent invulnerability of the ordained structure, the man at the top is a direct successor of the founder, Joseph Smith, the first prophet of the church. Rather like the role of the

Pope at the head of the Catholic Church, these Living Prophets can issue doctrinal edicts.

Where the Mormon Church differs from the Catholics is in its distribution of ownership. The structure may be hierarchical, but it is accessible. Anyone can be president. Anyone can be an apostle or any of the other spiritual roles within the church.[1] You do not have to be celibate, decked in black and red, or employed by the vast structure of the Vatican to run the church.

Where the Latter-day Saints also differ from the Catholic Church is that the management of the organization goes very wide and deep. The congregation runs itself. It administers moral, spiritual, and temporal benefits to the whole community and actively runs the organization. Within the entire church only the most senior leaders receive a stipend (the Apostles and the Seventy). Literally millions of people set aside strictly defined time commitments to help govern their individual religious communities. This degree of involvement is not just a matter of someone volunteering to arrange the church flowers, but is a direct substitute for the kind of responsibilities shouldered by paid clergy in other religions.

By creating a structure that encourages such wide and comprehensive distribution of responsibility and ownership amongst its members, is democratic (with a hint of the hand of God present), and totally involving for those who devote so much of their time and resources, the church has created a very robust organizational model. It remains to be seen (by our descendants I suspect) whether it is a more vigorous model than even the Catholic Church.

Similar to the Mormon Church, Mary Kay also employs an apparently daunting hierarchy. It begins with MK corporate and moves from national to regional to local directors of individual sales forces. Where it is radically different from most sales organizations however, is that Mary Kay is essentially a republic of independent businesses that pay a tithe up the line via other independent business owners to the Mary Kay Corporation. Each consultant is ultimately working for herself with the center only providing "spiritual direction" (especially in the form of the mythic founder) and the wherewithal to conduct their business in the form of products and sales materials.

Saturn distributes ownership to its retailers, each a separate fiefdom (notwithstanding that its buildings, its members' clothing, and its pricing policy is set to uniform standards). In fact, several of the "brand-defining" ideas would never have happened if it weren't for Saturn's culture of letting go. The now famous Saturn Cheer, where the retailers left what they were doing and clapped as a customer took delivery of their car, grew organically out of the retailer network.

At the factory, every line worker or member of management felt that they ran the company. Don Hudler, Saturn's second president, emphasized that Saturn, "adopted the philosophy early on, that everything we did, we would do by consensus." This was true even when it came to his own employment. He was interviewed not only by his management colleagues but also by union members.

By enacting such egalitarian and rare ideals, Saturn created a culture of mutual ownership that encouraged highly creative involvement in the brand. An authoritarian, rigidly enforced brand strategy and program would likely have missed the ideas that only a community freed to "play" would have generated. A distributed ownership within the body of the membership itself creates the right environment for ideas, energy, commitment, and ultimately advocates; a member who feels as if they have helped model the brand will likely be an evangelist for it.

Piggybacking

So the idea of sharing ownership with your community appeals to you, but you don't have a community yet? Don't despair. Just co-opt somebody else's. Piggybacking onto other communities has been a successful strategy of cult formation throughout history.

A nascent Christianity suckled from Judaism's breast, and the Mormons hopped onto Christianity's back. However, these are cult examples, and brands can't just appropriate the market leader (except by merger). As a fledgling shoe company, Nike couldn't just co-opt Adidas or its brand values, but it could, and did, leverage and own the emotions of the running community, and ultimately champion them. Ben & Jerry's couldn't latch onto Häagen-Dazs, but they could align themselves with the liberal agenda and gain market share off the back of the ideals of established political and social communities.

EBay is a cult that piggybacked itself into the business hall of fame. It latched onto preexisting communities of collectors. From the beginning they exploited the collecting culture by co-opting the collectors wherever they congregated. In 2000 alone, eBay had planned to sponsor or speak at forty-eight trade shows for collectors.[2] As one journalist explained, "The roots of this strategy for reaching into the collector community lie more in Tupperware parties than in the typical Internet model."[3] The "Tupperware party" idea was critical to eBay's growth since word-of-mouth marketing depends entirely on the reputation of the "evangelists" touting your services. In eBay's case, these evangelists were "collector-experts." EBay called them Ambassadors, and as George Koster, eBay's senior manager of new business, explained, their role was important for reaching the collecting population. "Collectors are like Amway distributors. They love what they're doing and they want to share it. We'll give [the Ambassadors] the tools so they can recruit others, so they can have parties in their houses and talk about eBay."

The French researchers Bernard and Veronique Cova wrote a paper on tribal marketing that proposes the doctrine of piggybacking.[4] They hold that marketers should consider their product or service from the perspective of its "linking" value to a community rather than its "use" value. That is, marketers need to ask how their brand can best *support* a community versus simply how the product is delivered and used by individual customers.

Cova and Cova note how Salomon, a very traditional ski brand was able to woo and grow market share within the snowboarding community. This was a difficult challenge given that the brand was hated by snowboarders. They were generally disparaged as "daddy's brand," preeminent in a sport of old farts: skiing. Realizing that they had an uphill battle, Salomon emphasized internally that it must "be humble" and that it had to "keep a low profile and listen."

This is a pretty radical strategy for marketers. Be humble? How often is that phrase uttered in the boardroom? But they pursued an infiltration plan by first observing snowboarders in their natural environment to learn their habits, needs, and attitudes. They created a marketing unit consisting of snowboarders and supported a team that didn't even use their brand (Salomon didn't make boards yet).

A year later, Salomon launched its new snowboard line with no advertising, simply a physical presence at training camps and the placement of Salomon boards in pro shops (not a traditional winter sports channel). They continued their strategy of community support by maintaining a presence at snowboarding playgrounds and allowing boarders to test out their products without any pressure to buy. They were just there, allowing the community to sample the product.

This strategy worked for Salomon, allowing it to rise to number three in the French snowboarding market within the same number of years. This feat is especially impressive considering that it didn't have the relatively easy task of launching a new brand. It was fighting the legacy of being a brand loathed by the very consumers that they were attempting to sell to. They achieved this feat by financing, supporting, and nurturing an existing community. They did not attempt to launch, attack, assualt, capture, or penetrate.

When piggybacking, it's vital to remember that the community is not something that is to be invaded. Nor do you employ all of the tactics and plans traditionally taught in marketing classes that more resemble battle plans to engage an enemy than approaches to engage a discriminating and independent community of customers. The community is more important than you or your brand. Loving the community and putting it first, so that it comes to adopt, own, and even champion your brand is the route to follow. Be ever so humble, for that is the way to gain lasting allegiance from your customer group.

Letting Go

It is tempting to interfere with your brand community, especially when things go wrong. BMW Motorcycles company almost ruined what started with the best of intentions. In a vivid example of learning the lesson of letting go, the brand team retreated, just in time, from the kind of bombastic interference redolent of command/control management.

They had provided a virtual church as a meeting place for its very independent community of riders. The company's communications agency, Merkley and Partners, turned what had been essentially a "brochureware" Web site into an actively used church hall where the running of services was left to the congregation. The new design recognized the community's obsession with the ride and made landscapes and riders the focus of the site. A ride section was designed, rather like a church notice board, where riders posted their favorite trips with maps and details for the rest of the community to use.

But the heart of the site consists of the bulletin boards in the actively used Community Section of the site. The site was the first by a major corporation to relinquish control of the content to the membership alone. It worked more like an independent organization's Web site than a company-sponsored one. This strategy worked well and the site was actively used. That is until about a month after launch, when a cult leader's (and major corporation's) fear came true. A disgruntled member started attacking the company.

He had a particular grudge. It wasn't until later that it was learned that he had applied for a job at BMW and was rejected. He started posting hate mail over the boards. He became a lightning rod for those who had had some bad experiences with the brand. Company officials were understandably nervous. Could they allow negative comments not only about the bike or a dealer or two, but also about the corporation to appear on a company Web site? After some debate, they believed they could not and instructed the agency pull all of the brand terrorist's postings off the board overnight.

This was the worst thing that they could have done. The company tried to control the boards and by doing so it lost control. The brand terrorist was elevated to martyr, and the company was made to look defensive. Many of the community who were neutral about the discontented rider's postings suddenly were not.

Quickly, the company reversed its decision. The negative comments were reposted and the marketing director made an announcement that in the future they would not censor the content, and that the boards would become self-policing. This would be the final company posting, he wrote, and he and other employees would only get on the boards in their capacity as fellow riders. The company retreated and the site now functions as a heavy traffic church for an active community with sixteen thousand registered users.

The BMW cult is run by the membership for the membership. Through a deft recovery, the company has enabled a highly functional sponsored meeting place for its decentralized cult and in the process built respect for itself from that membership. The delicate relationship between the company and its brand community was restored by its recognition that its role is one of support, not control.

Occasionally, gifts fall into the laps of unsuspecting brand managers. Sometimes communities will adopt a brand that the brand isn't trying to engage. If it does, don't mess with it. Resist your inclination to control events and let the community become the brand manager.

Timberland is one of these brands. Timberland is best known for their hiking boots and all their communications paint an authentic outdoor picture of the brand. Their retail outlets have the feel of wooden cabins and their Web site is laden with pictures of isolated natural beauty. Their "about Timberland" statement claims that they are the "global leader in the design of apparel and accessories for consumers who value the outdoors and their time in it." Yet Timberland boots are huge in the very urban hip-hop community. One rapper/producer has even named himself Timbaland, and in 2001 six boys were named for the brand. The company's revenue rose to $1.2 billion.

Alex Wipperfürth has written an excellent book called *Brand Hijack* that delves deep into this concept. One of his cases follows the story of Pabst Blue Ribbon (PBR), a popular blue-collar beer from Wisconsin. In the 1970s PBR was one of America's most popular beers, but its market share had declined ever since. Many factors caused this. For one, there were many shifts of company ownership and each new owner seemed content to let the brand slide. In an industry that annually spends roughly $1 billion advertising, PBR hasn't had a television campaign in many years.

Pabst, now owned by South African interests and based in San

Antonio, sold less than a million barrels in 2001. This was its lowest figure in decades and 90 percent below its peak in 1975. But by mid-2002 something had changed drastically. Pabst Blue Ribbon had miraculously become the fastest growing brand of all domestic beers, achieving double digit growth within a declining industry.

What happened to spark such a turnaround? A thriving community had adopted PBR as a brand that espoused their ideals. It started out West when the bike messenger community in Portland adopted Pabst as their beer. What they liked about the beer was much more than the fact that it typically sold for a dollar. They liked how they had never seen advertisements for it, and that it was a throwback to America's heartland and blue-collar ideals. It was a beer that wasn't about image.

Ironically, the bike messenger's embrace quickly gave PBR an image. They spurred a revolution that made PBR the rallying flag of urban hipsters everywhere. The *Hipster's Handbook*, a how-to guide for the hip-impaired declares PBR as, "The best-tasting domestic beer. Very popular with guys in work shirts and cowgirl hipsters. The only beer that is cool to drink out of the can." A trip to Williamsburg, Brooklyn (perhaps the epicenter of the hipster universe) easily cements the roots of PBR's comeback. Young counterculture ragamuffins with unwashed hair and torn jeans proudly wear Pabst T-shirts and hats. Almost every bar serves PBR and it has become the official beer of several art galleries.

Impressively, PBR's marketing team has resisted the temptation to jump on the hipster bandwagon and try to market to this cynical demographic. They realize that they are popular because they haven't been trying to woo anyone. Neal Stewart, PBR's divisional marketing manager, constantly uses such heretical phrases as, "let the consumer lead the brand," and "organic," or "genuine." When Kid Rock's camp was interested in an endorsement deal, Pabst declined. When offered the chance to sponsor major snowboarding events or support extreme athletes, it also passed. PBR wisely realizes that it needs to completely let go if they want to continue to enjoy their resurrection within the hipster community. To try and market to them would only be to offend them and therein lose their only constituency besides aging steelworkers.

Letting go is hard to stomach for most managers. The inclination to interfere is completely understandable given brand managers' job descriptions—ones that generally require skills for active command and control. I know. I, too, used to be in the middle of one of those brand manager–centric org charts at Procter and Gamble where the culture was one of direct action and consumer response.

Nonetheless, distribution of ownership is vital to ensure the cult's longevity and vigor. And sensitivity to one's role in a cult's management is critical as the community itself demands more participation in its destiny. The typical image of autocratic cult leader, or imperial brand manager is on its way out. A balance of power is on its way in.

CONCLUSION

The opportunity for creating cult brands has never been better. But at the same time the need to do so has never been more acute. Too many marketers have adopted a defensive attitude when actually they are on the brink of creating some of the most tenacious bonds between their brands and customers.

The smarter marketers have known for a long time that decisions for or against their brands are not just made rationally. In fact the smartest have known instinctively what neurologists now believe, that *no* decision is made entirely rationally. All decisions reference the emotional centers of the brain. They know that an emotional predisposition towards their brand can give them an advantage even when their product is out-featured or out-priced by competitors. Nonrational connections form the stickiest bonds.

Marketers' only real choice is to become more dependent on emotional ties or face ever-dwindling profits. As more markets are characterized by products and services with little material difference, brands have to become more central in satisfying emotional needs.

Few stronger emotions exist than the need to belong and make meaning. And brands are poised to exploit that need.

As we have seen, brands have the potential to become the new centers of community. They are the cousins of the newer types of communities that have replaced the old geographically anchored ones. Well financed and conceived, succored by media, communications, and mobility (the very things that eroded traditional communities), they can become the loci for groups of individuals unified by shared values, interests, and identity.

Whether by design or intuition, very few marketers (such as the ones we've studied) are doing the right things to exploit this opportunity. Others (the majority) are doing nothing and gaining nothing. And still others are enjoying the fruits of a strong community despite their inactivity (and in some cases because of it, such as Pabst and Timberland) because consumers have just got up and done it themselves.

I've studied cults because they are the most extreme manifestation of community, and I wanted to understand how devoted communities can be formed around brands. Some brands we've looked at are already enjoying dedication from their members. When someone can say, in all seriousness, "I think that there are people who would understand Macs and don't know it yet, and those are the people who have to be reached, those are the people *who have to be saved*," then clearly *brands already have the capacity to generate cultlike fanaticism.* The purpose of this book is to extend that capacity to many others.

Some people I've spoken to about this subject (including marketers) have been depressed at the prospect. "Is consumerism really going to penetrate so far into our lives that that the spawn of grubby business will replace the traditional ways of communing with our fellow citizens?" is the gist of their complaint. Others are skeptical that brands can satisfy such complex needs anyway. And others point to the growth of alternative forms of spirituality (yoga, Kabbala, Buddhism, etc.) as a sign that there's increasing disillusionment with the materialist American Dream.

These laments and skepticism may be justified. But based on the evidence of my and others' research, whether we like it or not, brands are being used as credible sources of community and meaning. And I think there's an important reason why they have been elevated to this role.

We live in a spiritual economy. There is a marketplace for worldviews and communities as well as goods and services. There are both consumers and producers of belief systems and community. And the laws of supply and demand apply as much in the spiritual exchange as they do in the economic. Where the economic and spiritual marketplaces differ, however, is that in the former, demand can rise and fall. In the spiritual marketplace demand is pretty constant. There is always a need to belong and make meaning. They are the essentials of the human condition after all.

Supply, however, can be satisfactory, plentiful, or entirely absent. When demand is satisfied, say, by vigorous organized churches with broad congregations, it is harder for new religions to edge their way into the marketplace. When it's not, you're likely to see many cults emerge. For example, the population of the Pacific coastal states are as religiously inclined as the rest of the country but they attend religious services much less, because there are fewer established Churches. As a relatively newly settled region with a highly transient population, traditional forms of worship have not yet taken root.[1] Alternatives are ready to spring up to meet the latent demand (an explanation for California's reputation as the source of wacky cults).

We may well be at a pivotal point in the supply/demand equation right now. The fact that significant numbers of people are looking to brands to provide the functions normally provided by social, religious, and political institutions is because those institutions are not meeting their needs. The traditional and established religious and secular institutions are having their authority questioned and their relevance reviewed by the general population.[2]

We've reached a unique intersection in society that favors marketers. On one side, established institutions are proving to be increasingly inadequate sources of meaning and community. On the other, there has been a growth of a very sophisticated kind of consumerism. Marketing is reaching its maturity in terms of shrewdness and artfulness. Billions are being spent on gratifying a discriminating audience with complex and subtly crafted brands. The confluence of these two trends is leading to these commercial creations being embraced by a population disillusioned by altogether less satisfying, and often less trusted organizations. Alongside alternative religions, brands are now serious contenders for belief and community.

So, as long as traditional institutions fail, and marketers remain sophisticated, then brands can become credible sources of community and meaning.

This is a major recalibration of the role of brands. And if you think you are exempt from the opportunity this presents because your product exists in an unexciting category (you sell packaged goods, for example, not motorcycles), that it is not especially competitive or has poor product performance, just remember that emotional attachment trumps rational analysis. At the end of the day, an Apple computer is just a box of electronics. While Harley has had a 40 percent market-leading share, it has also had a technically very poor product (they would leak oil on the showroom floor). We saw customers get passionate about, and generate complex identities for flavored sugar water, a "packaged good" that is consumed in minutes. Saturn has unexceptional cars, Mary Kay products are good but not revolutionary, and the WWF is absurd.

If you are resolved to start a cult brand, then here is a reminder of the most important principles of cult formation. Make your brand different enough, but the same enough. In the world of cult brands, people buy people, not things or ideas alone. Maintain just the right amount of tension with the norm. Have a meaning system, and an integrated system of symbology that communicates it. Invest at least as much into the cult as your members do in terms of emotional and financial commitment, energy, and creativity. Never lie. Rethink your position from being a commander-controller to being a community nurturer—a more humble role.

The next cult brand could be anything. The next cult brand could be yours.

NOTES

INTRODUCTION

1. *New York Times*, "Exurbia and God: Megachurches in New Jersey," by George James, June 29, 2003.

1. THE GREAT CULT PARADOX: WHY PEOPLE JOIN

1. Steve Hassan, *Combating Cult Mind Control*.
2. Eileen Barker, *The Making of a Moonie: Brainwashing or Choice?*
3. Robert Lifton, an eminent psychologist was commissioned by the U.S. government to investigate charges of brainwashing by the Chinese. His findings were published in *Thought Reform and the Psychology of Totalism*. He wrote the following in conclusion:

> Behind this web of semantic confusion lies an image of "brainwashing" as an all-powerful, irresistible, unfathomable and magical method of achieving total control over the human mind.
>
> *It is of course none of these things,* and this loose usage makes the word a rallying point for fear, resentment, urges toward submission, justification of failure, irresponsible accusations, and for a wide gamut of emotional extremism.

Additionally, mind control, brainwashing's cousin, has lost credibility as a manipulative cult technique as one of its most important proponents,

Margaret Thaler Singer, had her findings undermined by her own professional body, the American Psychology Association, when they found them to be "unsupportable."

3. WE LOVE YOU

1. Rodney Stark, *The Rise of Christianity*, p.19.
2. *Money Magazine*, April 2003.
3. Eileen Barker, *The Making of Moonie*; Mark Gallanter, *Cults: Faith, Healing, and Coercion*, 2nd Ed.
4. Mark Gallanter, *Cults*.
5. John Lofland and Rodney Stark, "Becoming a World-Saver: A Theory of Conversion to a Deviant Perspective," p. 871.

4. YOU BELONG

1. Lisa F. Berkaran, Ph.D.; Linda Leo-Summers MPH; Ralph I. Horowitz, M.D., *Emotional Support and Survival after Myocardial Infarction*, Annals of Internal Medicine, vol. 117, no. 12, 15 December 1992, pp. 1003–1009.
2. Peter Berger and Thomas Luckmann, *The Social Construction of Reality: A Treatise in the Sociology of Knowledge*, p. 51.
3. Muzafer Sherif documented the experiment in an influential work, *The Psychology of Social Norms*.
4. *Yankelovich Monitor*, Index 2002.
5. Robert Wuthnow. 1998. *Loose Connections: Joining Together in America's Fragmented Communities*, pg. 5
6. Albert Muniz and Thomas O'Guinn, "Brand Community," *Journal of Consumer Research*, March 2001.

5. CULTING IS A CONTACT SPORT

1. Mormon males—59 percent, females—64.4 percent versus the U.S. average for men—31.9 percent, and women—44.7 percent. From Douglas J. Davies, *Mormon Identities in Transition*, p. 48.
2. Dean Hoge and Fenggang Yang, "Determinants of Religious Giving

in American Denominations: Data from Two Nationwide Surveys," pp. 123–148.

3. The Church of Jesus Christ of Latter-day Saints, *Priesthood and Auxiliary Leaders' Guidebook*.

4. The Church of Jesus Christ of Latter-day Saints, *Teaching, No Greater Call: A Resource Guide for Gospel Teaching*.

5. The "Presidency" members receive a small stipend, but usually support themselves independently.

6. WE'RE IN THIS TOGETHER

1. Rodney Stark, *Rise of Christianity*.

2. Mary Kay Ash, *Mary Kay on People Management*.

7. THIS IS WHAT WE BELIEVE

1. The Body Shop brochure: "The Business of The Body Shop."

2. Jane Simons, *The Queen of Green*. Director, London. September 2000.

3. Christopher A. Bartlett, Kenton Elderin, and Krista McQuade, *The Body Shop International*, p. 4.

4. Anita Roddick, *Business as Unusual*.

5. Adam Morgan, *Eating the Big Fish*, pp. 169–170

6. Anita Roddick, *Business as Unusual*.

7. Ibid.

8. Elizabeth Lamoureux, *A Case Study of 'The Body Shops' Rhetoric of Corporate Social Responsibility*, p. 57

9. The Religious Movements Homepage: University of Virginia, http://religiousmovements.lib.virginia.edu

10. Charles W. Denison, "The Children of EST: A Study of the Experience and Perceived Effects of Large Group Awareness Training," Ph.D. Dis.

11. Anita Roddick, *Business as Unusual*.

8. SYMBOLISM

1. R. M. MacIver, *Society*, p. 340.

2. Wolfgang Koschnick, *Dictionary of Marketing*, p.40.

3. John Murphy, *Brand Strategy*, p. 18.
4. Rita Clifton and Esther Maughan, *Twenty-Five Visions: The Future of Brands*, p. 79.
5. James Auer, "Volkswagen exhibit fueled by style, German History," *Milwauwkee Journal Sentinel, Online Edition*, February 26, 2002.
6. Rita Clifton and Esther Maughan, *Twenty-Five Visions: The Future of Brands*, p. 71.

9. COMMITMENT IS A TWO-WAY STREET

1. Joanna and Chris, members of The Work whom I interviewed are equally angry about their lost sacrifice. As a result, they cooperate with a leading cult deprogrammer, Rick Ross, to publicize and inform on the highly secretive cult.
2. Jon Entine, "Shattered Image: Is The Body Shop Too Good to Be True?"
3. Jon Entine, "A Social and Environmental Audit of The Body Shop: Anita Roddick and The Question of Character."
4. As described to me by Rick Ross, one of the country's leading deprogrammers (or "exit counselors" as he described his trade).

10. GO FORTH AND MULTIPLY

1. From the "Articles of Faith of the Church of Jesus Christ of Latter-day Saints."

11. TENSION: THE MANAGEMENT OF DEVIANCE

1. Rodney Stark and William Sims Bainbridge *The Future of Religion: Secularization, Revival, and Cult Formation*.
2. Jan Shipps, *Mormonism: The Story of a New Religious Tradition*.
3. Both Kazaa and Altnet are owned by Sharman Networks.
4. Wendy Kaufman described herself as the anti-Christ of all advertising because she was five foot two and two hundred pounds in *Advertising Age*, June 23, 1997.
5. *The Wall Street Journal*, December 14, 1998.

6. *New York Times,* "Advertising," April 10, 1998.

7. *Advertising Age,* June 23, 1997.

13. THE CULT WAVERS, A CHURCH STRENGTHENS

1. Michael Bennett, Chairman of the UAW union local at Saturn from 1986 to 1999.

2. Keith Bradsher, "The Reality Behind the Slogan; Saturn Unit, once a Maverick, Is Looking a Lot More Like GM," *New York Times,* August 23, 2001.

14. WHO RUNS THE CULT?

1. However, there is one very big exception to this, one where the church has not responded to cultural pressure. These positions are only open to men.

2. Claire Tristram, "Takin' it to the Street," *MC Technology Marketing Intelligence,* February, 1999.

3. Ibid.

4. Bernard and Veronique Cova, "Tribal Marketing: The Tribalization of Society and Its Impact on the Conduct of Marketing," *European Journal of Marketing in 2002 and Beyond,* Version, January 2001.

CONCLUSION

1. Rodney Stark and William Sims Bainbridge discuss this in their excellent book *The Future of Religion: Secularization, Revival, and Cult Formation.*

2. Established churches in the West are seeing congregations shrink. In Europe, where many of the world faiths blossomed, attendance is in the low percentages of the population. In Britain, only 0.66 percent of the population attends the Church of England weekly. In France, only a paltry 5 percent attend a religious service every week, and even in Italy the percentage is as low as 15 percent and no higher than 33 percent (depending on which study you consult—"Faith Fades Where It Once Burned Strong," Frank Bruni, *New York Times,* November 13, 2003). Although the

United States is a more religious continent than Europe, the proportion of people who say that they never go to church or synagogue has tripled since 1972 to 33 percent in 2000, and those that do may be over-claiming. Professor of theology and culture, John G. Stackhouse, believes actual churchgoing "may be at little more than half the professed rate." Secular institutions are not doing so well either. The great foundations of our society that inform its collective identity do not currently get much of a vote from the American public, literally. Each election year a lower percentage of American voters turn out to vote than any other of the twenty-two established democracies in the world, except for Switzerland *(American Outlook Magazine)*. Only 18 percent of the public agree that they have "A great deal of confidence in" the American Judicial System, only 14 percent for the Federal Government, and 25 percent trust advice from lawyers. The institution of the presidency did a little better than lawyers at 30 percent. This survey was undertaken in mid-2003, just after a war allegedly fought in response to a threat of an attack on American citizens, normally a time when a country rallies around its civic institutions. People have most confidence in their "own abilities" which came in at 72 percent (2003 *Yankelovich Monitor*).

The influx of new religions is also a symptom of poor supply by domestic institutions. Where the major religions once functioned as one-stop shops for meaning and community, they are now competing for customers, many of whom are creating their own potpourris of belief, mixing a little Judaeo-Christian thought, with a touch of, say Buddhism and a sprinkling of tantric yoga. This behavior is happening because no single source is satisfying their needs.

BIBLIOGRAPHY

Adler, Alfred. 1956. *Individual Psychology of Alfred Adler: A Systematic Presentation in Selections from His Writings*, Heinz L. Ansbacher and Rowena R. Ansbacher, eds. New York: Basic Books.

Arens, William F. 1999. *Contemporary Advertising*, 7th ed. New York: Irwin McGraw-Hill.

Argyle, Michael and Beit-Hallahmi Benjamin. 1958. *The Social Psychology of Religion*. Boston: Routledge & Keegan Paul.

Ash, Mary Kay. 1984. *Mary Kay on People Management*. New York: Warner Books.

Baigent, Michael and Richard Leigh. 1989. *The Temple and the Lodge*. New York: Arcade Publishing.

Barger, Ralph "Sonny" with Keith and Kent Zimmerman. 2001. *Hell's Angel: The Life and Times of Sonny Barger and the Hell's Angels Motorcycle Club*. New York: Perennial.

Barker, Eileen. 1984. *The Making of a Moonie: Brainwashing or Choice?* Oxford: Basil Blackwell.

Bartlett, Christopher A., Kenton Elderin, and Krista McQuade. 1991. *The Body Shop International*. Cambridge, Mass.: Harvard Business School Publishing.

Batson, Daniel C., Patricia Schoenrade, and W. Larry Ventis. 1993. *Religion and the Individual: A Social-Psychological Perspective*. New York: Oxford University Press.

Bearden, William O. and Michael J. Etzel. 1982. "Reference Group Influence on Product and Brand Purchase Decisions." *Journal of Consumer Research* 9 (September): 183.

Bearden, William O., Richard G. Netemeyer, and Jesse E. Tell. 1989. "Measurement of Consumer Susceptibility to Interpersonal Influence." *Journal of Consumer Research* 15 (March): 474.

Bearden, William O. and Randall L. Rose. 1990. "Attention to Social Comparison Information: An Individual Difference Factor Affecting Consumer Conformity." *Journal of Consumer Research* 16 (March): 462.

Beresniak, Daniel. 1997. *Symbols of Freemasonry*. Paris: Editions Assouline.

Berger, Peter and Thomas Luckmann. 1966. *The Social Construction of Reality: A Treatise in the Sociology of Knowledge*. Garden City, N.Y.: Anchor Books.

Berkman, Lisa F., Ph.D.; Linda Leo-Summers MPH; and Ralph I. Horowitz, M.D. 1992. "Emotional Support and Survival after Myocardial Infaction," *Annals of Internal Medicine* (117, no. 12): 15 December 1003–1009.

Biedermann, Hans. 1989. *Dictionary of Symbols: Cultural Icons and the Meanings behind Them*. New York: Meridian.

Brasher, B. E. 1996. "Thoughts on the Status of the Cyborg: On Technological Socialization and Its Link to the Religious Function of Popular Culture." *Journal of the American Academy of Religion* 64, 4 (Winter): 809–30.

Bromley, David G. and Anson D. Schupe, Jr. 1979. *"Moonies" in America: Cult, Church, and Crusade*. Beverly Hills: Sage Publications.

Brown, Bridget. 2001. *The Terror Is Real: The History and Politics of Alien Abduction*. Ann Arbor, Mich., UMI Dissertation Services.

Buhler, Charlotte and Fred Massarik. 1968. *The Course of Human Life: A Study of Goals in the Humanistic Perspective*. New York: Springer Publishing Company.

Burnkrant, Robert E. and Alain Cousineau. 1975. *Informational and Normative Social Influence in Buyer Behavior. Journal of Consumer Research* 2 (December): 208.

Campbell, Joseph and Bill Moyers. 1988. *The Power of Myth*. New York: Broadway Books.

Carlilie, Richard. 1992. *Manual of Freemasonry*. Montana: Kessinger Publishing Company.

Carrier, Herve. 1965. *The Sociology of Religious Belonging*. New York: Herder and Herder.

Carter, David E. 1999. *Branding: The Power of Market Identity*. New York: Hearst Books.

Clifton, Rita and Esther Maughan. 2000. *Twenty-Five Visions: The Future of Brands*. New York: New York University Press.

Cole, Kenneth. 2003. *Footnotes*. New York: Simon & Schuster.

Collier, Gary. *The Cult of Christianity*. In press.

Cornwall, Marie. 1985. *Personal Communities: The Social and Normative Bases of Religion*. Ann Arbor, Mich.: UMI Dissertation Services.

Cova, Bernard and Veronique Cova. 2002. "Tribal Marketing: The Tribalization of Society and Its Impact on the Conduct of Marketing." *European Journal of Marketing: Special Issue Societal Marketing in 2002 and Beyond*. 36, no. 5: 595–620.

Dahlstrom, Sarah P. 1990. *The Uses of Evoked Experiences of Expanded Awareness in the Adult Woman's Search for Meaning and Purpose in Life*. Ann Arbor, Mich.: UMI Dissertation Services.

Daraul, Arkon. 1997. *A History of Secret Societies*. Seacaucus, N.J.: Citadel Press.

Darwin, Charles. 1859. *The Origin of Species*. New York: Bantam Books.

Davies, Douglas J., ed. 1996. *Mormon Identities in Transition*. London: Wellington House.

Dean, Roger A. 1992. *Moonies: A Psychological Analysis of the Unification Church*. New York: Garland Publishing.

Denison, Charles Wayne. 1994. *The Children of EST: A Study of the Experience and Perceived Effects of Large Group Awareness Training* (The Forum), Ph.D. Diss., University of Denver, Denver, Colorado.

Desormeaux, Lynne. 2000. *Meaning: Relationships to Coping Mechanisms and Well-Being*. Ann Arbor, Mich.: UMI Dissertation Services.

Deutsch, Morton and Harold Gerard. 1955. "A Study of Normative and Informational Social Influences upon Individual Judgment." *Journal of Abnormal and Social Psychology* 51: 629–36.

Deutschman, Alan. 2000. *The Second Coming of Steve Jobs*. New York: Broadway Books.

Dumenil, Lynn. 1984. *Freemasonry and American Culture 1880–1930*. Princeton, N.J.: Princeton University Press.

Bibliography

Eliade, Mircea. 1991. *Images and Symbols Studies in Religious Symbolism.* Princeton, N.J.: Princeton University Press.

Elliot, Aronson. 1999. *The Social Animal.* New York: Worth.

Elsner, J. and R. Cardinal. 1994. *The Cultures of Collecting.* Cambridge, Mass.: Harvard University Press.

Entine, Jon. 1994. "Shattered Image: Is The Body Shop Too Good to Be True?" *Business Ethics* Magazine, 8, no. 5: 23–28.

———. 1996. "A Social and Environmental Audit of The Body Shop: Anita Roddick and the Question of Character." www.jonentine.com

Etzioni, Amitai. 1993. *The Spirit of Community: The Reinvention of American Society.* New York: Simon & Schuster.

Finke, Roger and Rodney Stark. 1992. *The Churching of America 1776–1990: Winners and Losers in Our Religious Economy.* New Brunswick, N.J.: Rutgers University Press.

Fry, Prem S. and Paul T. P. Wong, eds. 1998. *The Human Quest for Meaning: A Handbook of Psychological Research and Clinical Applications.* Mahwah, N.J.: Lawrence Erlbaum Associates.

Gallanter, Mark. 1999. *Cults: Faith, Healing, and Coercion.* 2nd Ed. New York: Oxford University Press.

Giddings, Franklin H. 1908. *The Principles of Sociology.* New York: Macmillan.

———. 1923. *Readings in Descriptive and Historical Sociology.* New York: The Macmillan Company.

———. 1926. *Studies in the Theory of Human Society.* New York: The Macmillan Company.

Gladwell, Malcolm. 2000. *The Tipping Point: How Little Things Can Make a Big Difference.* Boston: Little Brown & Company.

Greeley, Andrew. 1982. *Religion: A Secular Theory.* New York: The Free Press.

Gross, Daniel. 1996. *Forbes Greatest Business Stories of All Time: 20 Inspiring Tales of Entrepreneurs Who Changed the Way We Live and Do Business.* New York: John Wiley & Sons.

Gusflied, Joseph R. 1975. *Community: A Critical Response.* New York: Harper & Row Publishers.

Hamilton, Malcolm B. 1995. *The Sociology of Religion.* London: Routledge.

Hammond, Philip E. 1985. *The Sacred in a Secular Age.* Berkeley, Cal.: University of California Press.

Hassan, Steve. 1988. *Combating Cult Mind Control.* Rochester, Ver.: Park Street Press.

Heinerman, John and Anson Shupe. 1985. *The Mormon Corporate Empire.* Boston: Beacon Press.

Heskett, James L., W. Earl Sasser, Jr., and Leonard A. Schlesinger. 1997. *The Service Profit Chain: How Leading Companies Link Profit and Growth to Loyalty, Satisfaction, and Value.* New York: The Free Press.

———. 2003. *The Value Profit Chain: Treat Employees like Customers and Customers like Employees.* New York: The Free Press.

Hoffer, Eric. 1951. *The True Believer: Thoughts on the Nature of Mass Movements.* New York: HarperCollins.

Hoge, Dean and Fenggang Yang. 1994. "Determinants of Religious Giving in American Denominations: Data from Two Nationwide Surveys." *Review of Religious Research* 36, 2 (December): 123–48.

Hongzhi, Li. 1999. *Falun Gong.* New York: The Universe Publishing NY Corporation.

Hopkins, Keith. 1999. *A World Full of Gods: Pagans, Jews and Christians in the Roman Empire.* London: Weidenfeld & Nicolson.

Jones, Arthur. 1977. *Malcolm Forbes: Peripatetic Millionaire.* New York: Harper & Row.

Kassarjian, Harold H. and Thomas S. Robertson. 1981. *Perspectives in Consumer Behavior.* Glenview, Ill.: Scott, Foreman and Company.

Katz, Donald. 1994. *Just Do It: The Nike Spirit in the Corporate World.* Holbrook, Mass.: Adams.

Keller, Ed and Jon Berry. 2003. *The Influentials.* New York: The Free Press.

Kelly, Joseph F. 1997. *The World of the Early Christians.* Collegeville, Minn.: The Liturgical Press.

Kinneman, John A. 1947. *The Community in American Society.* New York: Appleton-Century-Crofts, Inc.

Koschnick, Wolfgang. 1995. *Dictionary of Marketing.* Brookfield, Ver.: Gower Publishing Limited.

Lamoureux, Elizabeth. 1994. *A Case Study of "The Body Shops" Rhetoric of Corporate Social Responsibility.* Ann Arbor, Mich.: UMI Dissertation Services.

Leary, Janice Patricia. 1988. *The Relationship of Coping and Chronic Stress and*

Faith Development in Women: Mothers of Multihandicapped Children. Ann Arbor, Mich.: UMI Dissertation Services.

Lewis, James R. 1998. *The Encyclopedia of Cults, Sects, and New Religions.* Amherst, N.Y.: Prometheus Books.

Lifton, Robert Jay. 1961. *Thought Reform and the Psychology of Totalism: A Study of "Brainwashing" in China.* New York: W.W. Norton & Co.

Lindner, Eileen W. 2001. *Yearbook of American & Canadian Churches 2001: Considering Charitable Choice.* Nashville: Abingdon Press.

Lofland, John and Rodney Stark. 1965. "Becoming a World-Saver: A Theory of Conversion to a Deviant Perspective." *American Sociological Review* 30: 862.

MacIver, R. M. 1950. *Society.* New York: Macmillan.

Mackey, Albert Gallatin, William R. Singleton, and William James Hughan. 1905. *The History of Freemasonry.* New York: The Masonic History Company.

Mauss, Armand L. 1994. *The Angel and the Beehive: The Mormon Struggle with Assimilation.* Chicago: University of Illinois Press.

Mayhew, Henry. 1971. *The Mormons: Or Latter-day Saints.* New York: AMS Press.

Mead, Frank S. and Samuel S. Hill. Revised by Craig D. Atwood. 2001. *Handbook of Denominations in the United States.* 11th Ed. Nashville: Abingdon Press.

Melton, J. Gordon. 1992. *Encyclopedic Handbook of Cults in America.* New York: Garland Publishing.

Mol, Hans. 1976. *Identity and the Sacred.* New York: The Free Press.

Moon, Reverend Sun Myung. 1979. *Divine Principles.* Beverly Hills: Sage Publications.

Moore, Geoffrey A. 1991. *Crossing the Chasm: Marketing and Selling High-Tech Products to Mainstream Customers.* New York: HarperCollins.

Morgan, Adam. 1999. *Eating the Big Fish.* New York: John Wiley & Sons, Inc.

Mullen, Robert. 1966. *The Latter-Day Saints: The Mormons Yesterday and Today.* Garden City, N.Y.: Doubleday & Company, Inc.

Muniz, Albert. M. Jr. and Thomas C. O'Guinn. 2001. "Brand Community." *Journal of Consumer Research,* 27 (March): 412–432

Murphy, John. 1990. *Brand Strategy.* New York: Prentice Hall.

Oppenheimer, Louis and Jaan Valsiner. 1991. *The Origins of Action: Interdisciplinary and International Perspectives*. New York: Springer-Verlag.

Osborn, Loran David and Martin Henry Neuermeyer. 1933. *The Community and Society: An Introduction to Sociology*. New York: American Book Company.

Papotto, Frank Joseph. 1991. *The Role of Self-Awareness, Certainty and Social Support in a Group Pressure Situation*. Ann Arbor, Mich.: UMI Dissertation Services.

Pargament, Kenneth I. 1997. *The Psychology of Religion and Coping: Theory, Research, Practice*. New York: The Guilford Press.

Park, C. Whan and V. Parker Lessig. 1977. "Students and Housewives: Differences in Susceptibility to Reference Group Influence." *Journal of Consumer Research* 4 (September): 103.

Piatigorsky, Alexander. 1997. *Freemasonry: The Study of a Phenomenon*. London: The Harvill Press.

Pinker, Steven. 2002. *The Blank Slate: The Modern Denial of Human Nature*. New York: Viking.

Porter, Kelley A. 1999. *eBay, Inc.* Boston: Harvard Business School Publishing.

Putnam, Robert D. 2000. *Bowling Alone: The Collapse and Revival of American Community*. New York: Simon & Schuster.

Reichheld, Frederick F. 1990. *The Quest for Loyalty: Creating Value through Partnership*. Boston: Harvard Business School Press.

———. 1996. *The Loyalty Effect: The Hidden Force behind Growth, Profits, and Lasting Value*. Boston: Harvard Business School Press.

Roberts, Richard H. 1995. *Religion and the Transformation of Capitalism: Comparative Approaches*. New York: Routledge.

Roddick, Anita. 2000. *Business as Unusual*. London: Thorsons.

Roof, Wade Clark. 1999. *Spriritual Marketplace: Baby Boomers and the Remaking of American Religion*. Princeton, N.J.: Princeton University Press.

Rouner, Leroy S., ed. 1991. *On Community*. Notre Dame, Ind.: University of Notre Dame Press.

Rothenberg, Randall. 1995. *Where the Suckers Moon*. New York: Vintage Books.

Sacharin, Ken. 2001. *Attention! How to Interrupt, Yell, Whisper, and Touch Consumers*. New York: John Wiley & Sons, Inc.

Bibliography

Sherif, Muzafer. 1936. *The Psychology of Social Norms.* New York: Harper.

Sherman, Joe. 1994. *In the Rings of Saturn.* New York: Oxford.

Shipps, Jan. 1985. *Mormonism: The Story of a New Religious Tradition.* Chicago: University of Illinois Press.

———. 2000. *Sojourner in the Promised Land: Forty Years among the Mormons.* Chicago: University of Illinois Press.

Simms, Jane. 2000. *The Queen of Green.* London, Director.

Simpson, Jeffry A. and Douglas T. Kenrick. 1997. *Evolutionary Social Psychology.* Mahwah, N.J.: Lawrence Erlbaum Associates.

Singer, Margret Thaler and Janja Lalich. 1995. *Cults in Our Midst: The Hidden Menace in Our Everyday Lives.* San Fransisco: Jossey-Bass.

Smith, Eliot R. and Diane M. Mackie. 2000. *Social Psychology.* Philadelphia: Macmillan.

Stafford, James A. 1966. "Effects of Group Influences on Consumer Brand Preferences." *Journal of Marketing Research.* 3 (February): 69.

Stark, Rodney. 1997. *The Rise of Christianity.* San Francisco: HarperCollins.

Stark, Rodney and William Sims Bainbridge. 1985. *The Future of Religion: Secularization, Revival, and Cult Formation.* Berkeley: University of California Press.

Stark, Werner. 1972. *The Sociology of Religion: The Study of Christendom.* London: Routledge and Kegan Paul.

Steiger, Brad and Hayden Hewes. 1997. *Inside Heaven's Gate: The UFO Leaders Tell Their Story in Their Own Words.* New York: Signet.

Strasser, J. B. and Laurie Beckland. 1991. *Swoosh: The Unauthorized Story of Nike and the Men Who Played There.* Orlando, Flor.: Hardcourt Brace Jovanovich.

Stross, R. E. 2000. *eBoys.* New York: Crown Publishers.

Swingewood, Alan. 1992. *A Short History of Sociological Thought.* 2nd Edition. Hong Kong: Macmillan.

The Body Shop. *The Business of The Body Shop,* brochure.

The Church of Jesus Christ of Latter-day Saints. 1978. *Gospel Principles.* Salt Lake City: The Church of Latter-day Saints.

———. 1981. *The Book of Mormon: Another Testament of Jesus Christ.* Salt Lake City: The Church of Latter-day Saints.

———. 1999. *Teaching, No Greater Call: A Resource Guide for Gospel Teaching.* Salt Lake City: The Church of Latter-day Saints.

———. 2001. *Priesthood and Auxiliary Leaders' Guidebook.* Salt Lake City: The Church of Latter-day Saints.

Thompson, Hunter S. 1966. *Hell's Angels.* New York: Ballantine Books.

Watt, William Montgomery. 1963. *Truth in the Religions: A Sociological and Psychological Approach.* Chicago: Adeline Publishing Company.

Whalen, William J. 1964. *The Latter-Day Saints in the Modern Day World.* New York: The John Day Company.

Wilson, Colin. 2000. *The Devil's Party: A History of Charlatan Messiahs.* London: Virgin.

Winans, Christopher. 1990. *Malcolm Forbes: The Man Who Had Everything.* New York: St. Martin's Press.

Wipperfürth, Alex. In Press. *Brand Hijack: The Rise of the Market Driven Brand.*

Wuthnow, Robert. 1987. *Meaning and Moral Order: Exploration in Cultural Analysis.* Berkeley: University of California Press.

Wuthnow, Robert. 1994. *"I Come Away Stronger": How Small Groups Are Shaping American Religion.* Grand Rapids, Mich.: William B. Eerdmans Publishing Company.

Wuthnow, Robert. 1998. *Loose Connections: Joining Together in America's Fragmented Communities.* Cambridge, Mass.: Harvard University Press.

Vallacher, Robin R. and Daniel M. Wegner. 1985. *A Theory of Action Identification.* Hillsdale, N.J.: Lawrence Erlbaum Associates.

Vogt, Ogden V. 1951. *Cult and Culture: A Study of Religion and American Culture.* New York: Macmillan.

Yankelovich Monitor Index, 2002.

Yankelovich Monitor Index, 2003.

Yates, Brock. 1999. *Outlaw Machine: Harley-Davidson and the Search for the American Soul.* Boston: Little Brown & Company.

INDEX

Index

Index

Index

Index

Index